CONFESSIONS
OF CUSTARD
A Military Mule

CONFESSIONS OF CUSTARD
A Military Mule

Letters to Merrie and Bright
1929-1932

by
V.R. Burkhardt

LEO COOPER
LONDON

First published in Great Britain in 1995 by
LEO COOPER
190 Shaftesbury Avenue, London WC2H 8JL
an imprint of
Pen & Sword Books Ltd,
47 Church Street,
Barnsley, South Yorkshire S70 2AS

A CIP record of this book is available from the British
Library

IBSN 0 85052 490 3

Printed in England by
Redwood Books Ltd
Trowbridge, Wilts.

Foreword

In 1983 I wrote a book in conjunction with the Imperial War Museum entitled *Animals in War*. Few subjects that I have written about have moved me quite as much as this. One talks of man's inhumanity to man but what about our inhumanity to animals? Did you know that 326,073 horses died during the Boer War, mainly from disease or that the Russians sent specially trained dogs to run under tanks with mines strapped to their bodies?

Among the many species of animals and birds co-opted by the soldiery, few touched my heart more than the mules. Because they had great character and minds of their own, they acquired a totally unfair reputation for obstinacy and bloody-mindedness. Yet their drivers, or muleteers, loved them, cherished them and in many cases died for them. As beasts of burden what they were required to do was almost beyond comprehension. They could go where no vehicle could go, they required scant sustenance, they were stong and brave and, in most cases, obedient. Anyone who has watched the recent programmes on the television about the Chindits in Burma will recall the dreadful pictures of the country that these loyal animals had to cross. At the same time, one must remember too how hard they worked in the Great War and indeed also in Italy during the Second World War and in many other theatres.

Custard was perhaps lucky. As far as we know she never saw action but was, nevertheless, an integral part of a Royal Field Artillery Unit (between those two wars). She was clearly a great character, gentle enough with children but not averse to a bit of eccentric behaviour. In Colonel Burkhardt (alias Custard)'s charming letters to his little friends Merrie and Bright we have a classic example of that great British skill, anthropomorphism.

Witty, observant and brilliantly illustrated, Custard's alter ego rules the day. This book, I hope, will be seen as a tribute to all mules who served in the armed forces and in particular to Custard herself — a specially talented mule whose pen was mightier than the sword and whose drawings are reminiscent of Tenniel. A wonderful book.

Jilly Cooper

Introduction

In 1928 the writer of the letters in this book, Major V.R. Burkhardt, DSO, OBE, returned from five years in China to Regimental duties at home, commanding the 13th Light Battery, 5th Light Brigade R.A. at Ewshott in Hampshire. He found his second-in-command was my father, Captain 'Ack-Ack' Middleton. My sister and I – then six and five – were nicknamed Merrie and Bright after a favourite song from 'The Arcadians'.

Early in 1929 our family moved from Farnham to *Los Pinos*, Reading Road, Fleet, quite close to the barracks. My mother was expecting another child in April so my father took Bright and me to Church Parade every Sunday – a short, cheerful service with the hymns taken at a good galloping pace. Afterwards we went with the officers to inspect 'the Lines' where the mules were kept. We walked through the stables talking to the mules whose names began with the letter of their sub-section – like Abel, Babs, Cora, and old Dan who, unusual for a mule, had a cross marking on his back. Mules are as temperamental as opera singers, none more so than Cora who won a lot of prizes but was apt to lay back her ears, bare her teeth, show the whites of her eyes and kick out. We gave her a wide berth and hurried on to our favourite yellow mule – Custard – who was almost always friendly and gentle, but could be as obstinate as her donkey father. Lieutenant Davies – 'Mr Davie' – took her out of her stall, we were put up bare-back and led to the Officers' Mess where the mess steward brought out carrots and sugar lumps for us to give to Custard. The officers stood around joking and teasing while we chattered and asked endless questions. Getting Custard back to her stable was difficult and took several officers pulling and pushing while we walked backwards, holding out enticing sugar lumps on the palms of our hands.

Because of her age and the state of her knees, Custard was no longer a member of a team pulling gun carriages. She had been demoted to carrying the reels of signal cable or baggage, but above all kept on for her entertainment value, not only to us but as an honorary member of the Officers' Mess, which she regularly attended on guest nights. Guests, and arriving or departing officers, were put up and 'shrugged' or bucked off.

Sunday was the best day of the week for us; not only did we visit Custard but we actually had Daddy almost to ourselves. We had seen very little of him in India where he was away for months at a time on exercises or manoeuvres, and he was at his jovial best in the company of his fellow officers. We also had dining-room lunch which was a great improvement on the habitually disgusting nursery food,

About Easter we started drawing pictures and writing letters to Custard; later, Custard started sending letters with pictures to us. This was no surprise as all our books – the *Just-So Stories*, *The Jungle Book*, *The Wind in the Willows*, and *Alice in Wonderland* – were about animals who spoke as humans. It was a surprise to our mother who thought Major Burkhardt (no-one knew his Christian name) 'rather a dull chap'. He was older and more reserved than the ebullient young officers she had met in India, where they danced, played golf and tennis, rode and hunted jackal. Now she found that he had hidden – at least from her – wit, learning and considerable talent as a draughtsman, on a different level from other Gunner officers trained at 'the Shop' – the Royal Military Academy, Woolwich.

I started having asthma attacks after visiting the stables or stroking the family dogs and cat. While propped up in bed inhaling Friar's Balsam, and missing being a bridesmaid, I was greatly consoled by Custard's sympathetic letters, especially as allergies were not then recognised and my mother said I was 'just timid'. I felt I was not a proper soldier's daughter like my fearless and mischievous little sister.

In 1931 we moved to Catterick, and 13th Battery with Major Burkhardt and Custard moved to Bulford; but we and Custard kept on writing till 'the Major' went back to China in 1932. We never saw him or Custard again but our mother treasured the letters and showed them to all her grand-children and great grand-children. 'Ack-Ack' and 'the Major' kept in touch and met several times in 'the Rag' – the Army and Navy Club – during the Second World War. In 1963 my father, by now a retired Brigadier, was killed in a car crash. 'The Major' now a retired Colonel in Hong Kong, wrote a letter of sympathy. In her reply my mother mentioned that she still had the letters, and in another letter in 1966, Colonel Burkhardt wrote: 'Fancy Custard's confessions having survived! I was supremely lucky to inherit 13 after Ack had breathed his spirit into the Battery. I had nothing to do but to sit back and benefit while devoting myself to juvenile literature. Custard's confessions were always easier to write after a visit from the children, for their questions provided material for the answers'.

I remember 'the Major' having a kind, dark face, gently smiling, standing slightly apart, saying little but clearly missing nothing. After his death in 1967, a Hong Kong friend, J.R. Jones, who as a wartime gunner, had first met him in France in the autumn of 1915, wrote in his obituary: 'He was a man of great personal charm and amiability. He had the bearing and pride of the distinguished professional soldier, one of nature's true gentlemen, while his gift of languages, his wide knowledge, sense of humour, and unusually retentive memory made him a most interesting raconteur'. Bright and I would like the publication of these letters to serve as a belated thanks and memorial to him − and of course, we have never forgotten dear old Custard.

M.A.M.J.

Above: *L to R* Major Burkhardt, Lieutenant Davies, Custard with Bright and Merrie, Major F.H. Richards, DSO.

Above: 13th Light Battery (Major Burkhardt in Mufti).

Below: 13th Light Battery.

R.A. MESS,
EWSHOTT CAMP,
Nº ALDERSHOT,
HANTS.

25ᵗʰ AUGUST 1929

MY DEAR BRIGHT

I AM AFRAID

I HAVE FALLEN FROM GRAGE, (AND ON THE OTHER KNEE THIS TIME) SO I AM LOOKING OUT FOR A JOB AS HOUSE-MAID, WHICH I HEAR IS THE ONLY PROFESSION IN WHICH BIG KNEES ARE FASH--IONABLE.   I DO SO HOPE

11

THE MODES WILL CHANGE, AND
LONG SKIRTS WOULD COME BACK,
THEN I COULD GO IN FOR A
REAL TOURNAMENT (NOT TENNIS)

BUT

SOMETHING LIKE THE. THEN I
COULD LET MY HAIR GROW INSTEAD
OF HAVING IT BOBBED BY SERGEANT
EDWARDS. IT USED TO
BE RATHER A NICE AUBURN

COLOUR, BUT HE SAID IT WAS
CARROTY. NOW I KNOW WHAT
CARROTS ARE AS WELL AS ANY-
BODY, AND IT WASN'T A BIT
LIKE THAT. WHEN IT IS AL-
LOWED TO GROW AGAIN I SHALL
PUT SOME STUFF ON TO MAKE IT
GOLDEN. AND THEN I'LL EASILY
GET A JOB
AS A
BARMAID

I WOULDN'T MIND
HAVING A GLASS
WITH YOU MYSELF
IF YOU DROP
IN

ALWAYS

"CUSSY" TO YOU

DEARIE :

R. A. MESS,
EWSHOTT CAMP,
Nº ALDERSHOT,
HANTS.

MY DEAR BRIGHTIE

IN READING MY

"OBSERVER" ON SUNDAY

I CAME ACROSS A POEM
ABOUT YOU _ SO I THOUGHT
I'D SEND IT ALONG AS
'T WASN'T LONG

"THERE WAS A YOUNG LADY CALLED
BRIGHT
WHO TRAVELLED MUCH FASTER
THAN LIGHT

SHE STARTED ONE DAY

IN A RELATIVE WAY

AND CAME BACK THE PREVIOUS
NIGHT.

! DO HOPE YOU'RE NOT SO FAST AS THAT FOR I'M RATHER OLD FASHIONED . AND HAVE NEVER BEEN IN A MOTOR CAR YET.

AND THAT REMINDS ME I HAVE'NT SEEN YOU FOR DONKEY'S YEARS WHICH ARE (RELATIVELY), FOR WE ARE RELATED, LONGER THAN MULES EARS

" 'EAR 'EAR " SAYS SHE WAGGING THEM BOTH

YOUR OLD ' CUS '

R. A. MESS,
EWSHOTT CAMP,
Nᴿ ALDERSHOT,
HANTS.

25ᵀᴴ SEPTEMBER 1929

MY DEAR MERRIE

WHAT DISGUSTING LUCK THAT WE BOTH MISSED THE WEDDING. I SHOULD HAVE LOVED TO HAVE CARRIED YOU AND BRIGHT THROUGH AN ARCH OF SWORDS, BUT AS YOUR BIG DADDY WAS'NT THERE THE LITTLE OFFICERS LIKE Mᴿ DAVEY WOULD HAVE HAD TO STAND ON TUBS TO MAKE THEM TALL ENOUGH FOR US TO PASS THROUGH.

I HAD TO STAY BEHIND TO LOOK AFTER THE OTHER MULES AS ALL THE OFFICERS WERE AWAY THAT DAY. OTHERWISE

WHEN I HEARD YOU WERE NOT
COMING I OFFERED TO PULL
THE MOTOR CAR WITH HAZEL
AND M?. WILLANS FROM THE
CHURCH TO THE HOTEL

BUT THEY SAID THE STREETS WERE

TO CROWDED. NOW YOU ARE WELL
AGAIN I DON'T MIND TELLING YOU
HOW DISAPPOINTED I WAS AND I
THINK IT WAS WORSE FOR ME THAN
FOR YOU. YOU SEE YOU'LL HAVE
LOTS MORE CHANCES OF BEING

A  BRIDESMAID. BUT

I SHALL NEVER

BE ABLE TO

WEAR

THAT ROSETTE

I HAD SET MY

HEART ON, AS

THEY

WON'T GIVE ME

ONE AT THE SHOW. COME
AND SEE ME TO CHEER ME UP
YOUR DEJECTED OLD
CUSTARD

"C" SUB. STABLE
13TH LIGHT BATTERY
EWSHOTT

5TH. OCTOBER 1929

MY DEAR MERRIE

I AM SO VERY,

SORRY TO HEAR YOU'RE ILL.

I DO WISH YOU'LL SOON GET WELL
AND TALKING OF WISHING WELL, I
HEAR YOU AND BRIGHT FOUND A
WISHING WELL THE OTHER DAY.

I WAS COMING BACK FROM MANOEUVRES THE OTHER DAY AND WE CAME TO A PLACE CALLED WELL. I WAS VERY THIRSTY AND THOUGHT IT WAS ABOUT TIME FOR MY "ELEVENSES" SO I STOPPED OUTSIDE A PUBLIC HOUSE.

DO YOU KNOW WE'D STARTED SO EARLY THAT THE PLACE WASN'T OPEN, AND I COULD'NT GET MY GLASS OF ALE. THEY REALLY OUGHT TO HAVE TIME-TABLES FOR THESE PLACES. I DON'T KNOW WHAT ENGLAND IS COMING TO. IT WASN'T AS IF I HADN'T BEEN A BONA FIDE TRAVELLER WHICH DOESN'T MEAN FIDO WITH A BONE, BUT IS GREEK OR LATIN FOR THE KIND OF TRAVELLER I AM. WELL, I THOUGHT AS THE PLACE WAS CALLED WELL THERE MUST BE A WELL IN IT, AND

IF THERE WAS I'D GET MY NOSE WELL IN.
SURE ENOUGH THERE WAS A WELL, AND
A SEAT TO SIT ON, BUT THE WELL WAS
BRICKED UP AND I COULD FIND NOTHING
BUT A TAP BELONGING TO THE WATER
COMPANY AND NO KEY TO TURN IT
ON.

I WAS SO ANGRY THAT I WALKED
STRAIGHT INTO A BIG POND AND GOT
MY SHOES ALL WET.

Do you know I'm quite jealous. I hear
you and Bright forgot yourselves so
far as to ride on a man's back in
Norway. Now that may be all right
for a savage foreign country, but when
you're in England remember that you
can only be carried by

Your old "Cus"

R. A. MESS,
EWSHOTT CAMP,
Nᴿ ALDERSHOT,
HANTS.

OCTOBER 1929

MY DEAR BRIGHT

THE MAJOR HAS GONE
BACK TO SCHOOL SO I
CAN SIT DOWN AND WRITE
YOU A NICE LONG LETTER.

WITHOUT BEING DISTURBED

I REALLY LOOK
POSITIVELY
HERALDIC
WRITING A
LETTER.

YOU CAN'T THINK WHAT A
NUISANCE THAT MAN IS, IN
THE TRAINING SEASON WHEN
I HAVE TO RUN OUT THE
TELEPHONE WIRE FOR HIM, AND
CAN'T STOP TO PICK DAISIES.
HE ALWAYS WANTS THE

TELEPHONE MULE

PUSHED WELL TO THE FRONT.

LAST WEEK I CAME INTO THE MESS AFTER DINNER TO SAY GOOD BYE TO SOME OF THE OFFICERS AND CLERGYMEN WHO WERE GOING AWAY. THEY ALL GOT ON MY BACK FOR A LAST RIDE, BUT SOME BODY TIED THE PADRE'S COAT TAILS UNDER MY TAIL. I SUPPOSE HE MEANT TO BE KIND AND FIX HIM ON, BUT I THOUGHT I'D LIKE TO GIVE HIM A GOOD SEND OFF. SO

I JUST SHRUGGED MY SHOULDERS
AND THEY ALL FELL OFF.

I THINK THE PADRE OUGHT TO
RIDE "DAN" BECAUSE HE'S GOT
A CROSS ON HIS BACK.

"DAN"

YOUR LOVING

CUSTARD

R. A. MESS,

EWSHOTT CAMP,

Nᴿ ALDERSHOT,

HANTS.

21ˢᵗ OCTOBER 1929

MY DEAR BRIGHT

THE CLIPPING SEASON HAS

BEGUN

AND THEY'VE TAKEN OFF MY FUR COAT.
I DON'T REALLY MIND AS IT WAS
SO HOT OUT WALKING, AND THEY GIVE

US TWO LOVELY RUGS IN THE STABLE. WE HAVE GREAT GAMES WITH THEM, AND WHEN THEY GET SHABBY, WE JUST PULL THEM OFF AND EAT THEM. I KNOW YOU'LL ASK WHAT THEY'RE LIKE TO EAT, SO

I MAY AS WELL TELL THEY'RE LIKE HAY NETS, OR CHEWING STRING. THEY'RE FRIGHTFULLY FULL OF VITAMINS, AT LEAST MINE ARE, AFTER I'VE BEEN WEARING THEM FOR SOME TIME. ONLY, YOU MUST NEVER EAT THE BUCKLE! IT HAS NO FOOD VALUE ANYWAY, AND THE SERGEANT ALWAYS SEEMS TO WANT IT. I BELIEVE HE COLLECTS THEM, BUT HE SAY HE CAN EXCHANGE THEM WITH THE "ORDNANCE" FOR NEW RUGS. THE "ORDNANCE" MUST BE A BIT OF A BARRACK MUG IF HE DOESN'T KNOW THE DIFFERENCE BETWEEN A RUG AND A BUCKLE.

CORA MADE AN AWFUL FUSS WHEN THEY
TRIED TO TAKE HER COAT OFF. LAST
TIME SHE LOOKED AS IF HER HAIR HAD
BEEN CUT WITH A KNIFE AND FORK —

OR NIBBLED BY A GOAT !
I SPOKE TO HER ABOUT BEING SO FIDGETY
AND SHE CALLED ME AN OLD YELLOW CAT.
NOW I'M NOT A BIT CATTY AM I ?
OLD "CROKE'S" FACE CERTAINLY HAS
ALL THE MALIGNITY OF A TOM·CAT
WITHOUT HIS SINGLENESS
OF PURPOSE —

HE BIT THE FARRIER THE OTHER DAY
WHILE HE WAS DRESSING MY WOUNDS AFTER
LAST MANOEUVRES

I THINK YOU'D ALWAYS BETTER KEEP ON
DAN'S SIDE WHEN YOU COME INTO MY STALL
TO SEE ME

ALWAYS AND EVER

YOUR OLD

Cussy.

TELEPHONE,
FLEET 67.

R.A.MESS,
EWSHOTT CAMP,
Nᵉ ALDERSHOT,
HANTS.

25 th OcTOBER I92 9

MY d EAR MERRIE

I AM LEARNING THE
TYP EWRiTER AS I
THINK EVERY GIRL
N●Wadays shOULD hAVE
SOME SORT OF
PROFE●SION.
Y●U SEE IT
WILL BE VERY
usEFuL t● ME WHEN I LEAVE THE ARMY
⌐$'M nOT VErY CERTAIN YET ABOUT ALl

THESE CAPiTAL$ ANd FiGURES aNd the
DOLLAR SiGN IS SO LIKE AN "S" ThAT I
SOMETIM$ PUT HIM IN BY MI$TAKE - THERE
I DID IT THEN ! I THOUGHT IN ABOut
SIX MonTH'S TIME I WOULD SEE IF I could-
d'NT PASS AN ExAminATION, AND GET MY
PROFICIENCY PAY By HELPING THE BATTERY
ClERK IN THE OFFICE. HE SAYS HE'S
VERY BUSY WITH DRAFTS JUST NOW. I
ALWAYS THOUGHT DRAFTS WAS

SOME SORT

OF

GAME,

BUT HE SAYS THEY'RE NO JOKE.
PERHAPS HE'S NOT A VERY GOOd P LAYER.

WE ARE JUST BEGINNINg OUR ANNUAL RAT
WEEK? AND THE RATS ARE DIGGING THEM-
SELVES IN.   THEY HAVE ALL GOT
THEIR LITTLE WHITE APRONS ON AND

are AS BUSY AS MOLES.   YOU SEE THE
GOVERNMENT TeLLS US THAT THEY STEAL
SO MUCH OF OUR CORN THAT WE MUST
HUNT THEM AT LEAST ONCE A YEAR.   WE
HAVE TO REPORT HOW MANY We HAVE
CAUGHT, AND HOW WE DID IT.   THEY
GIVE U$ TRAPS, BUT WE HAVE TO FIND
THE CHEESE OURSELVES.
        MR. DAVIE HAD THE HEAD CAT UP

IN THE BATTERY OFFICE, AND TOLD HIM
TO GET ON WITH THE JOB.

HE TOLD HIM OFF PROPERLY, AND
SAID THAT HE'D DOCK HIS PROFICIENCY
PAY, AND TAKE   AWAY   HIS   STRIPES

R.A. MESS,
EWSHOTT CAMP,
Nᴿ ALDERSHOT,
HANTS.

RATION STORE

IF HE CAUGHT HIM LOAFING ROUND THE

MEAT STORE AGAIN.

I DON'T THINK THAT CAT WOULD LOOK

VERY WELL WITHOUT STRIPES.

HE'S A REGULAR OLD SOLDIER THOUGH,
AND PUT ALL THE BLAME ON THE RATS. HE
SAID AS THEY DIDN'T SUBMIT AN A.F.
B 2I3 SHOWING WEEKLY INCREASE AND
DECREASE, HIS FIGURES COULD ONLY BE
APPROXIMATE.   HE SAID HE COULDN'T
TRUST SOME OF THE YOUNGER KITTENS
NOT TO EAT THE RATS WITHOUT REPORTING
TO HIM.

I WAS PLEASED TO GET THAT LETTER
FROM YOU, AND THINK YOU DRAW CATS MUCH
BETTER THAN I DO.   PERHAPS IT COMES
OF KEEPING A CAT IN THE HOUSE.

CORA WAS WILD WITH JEALOUSY WHEN
SHE SAW THE LETTER ADDRESSED TO
        "THE HONOURABLE"   SHE SAID SHE
HAD AS MUCH RIGHT TO THE "R.A." AS

I HAD? BUT I PUT HER IN HER PLACE BY
SAYING IN HER CASE IT MEANT

    "RARELY AMIABLE"

  I THINK I'VE CONQUERED THAT $
TRICK

     YOUR LOVING

       CU$$ → CUS.

TELEPHONE,
FLEET 67.

R. A. MESS,
EWSHOTT CAMP,
Nᴿ ALDERSHOT,
HANTS.

27th October 1929

My Dear BRIGHT

Do   You   know
I really believe
that there is
    a good chance
of my becoming a

CINEMA STAR !

Of course I don't
mean one of these

41

things that are all teeth and

hair

Like a Ratcatcher's Dog, but a
real proper actress with a part
of my own.

About two months ago an old
gentleman came up to see the Major
and wanted to make a film of a
LIGHT BATTERY at work, and of
course as we'd won all these prizes
at the Horse Show he came to us.

He particularly wanted a
special picture of the Telephone

Mule, doing the Signalling, and there
is only BRONCHO and me in the Battery
that knows anything about it.   So
you see it must be one of us that is
chosen

BRONCHO was very "bobbery" the last
day at Camp, and nearly got left
behind, so I hope they'll chose me.

I am practising Semaphore hard
and can send quite well now as you
will see

Your loving
C U S.

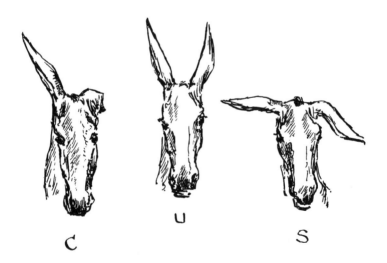

C   U   S

TELEPHONE.
FLEET 67.

R. A. MESS,
EWSHOTT CAMP,
Nᵣ ALDERSHOT,
HANTS.

P.S.

I think if you put in a word
with Mr. Davie he might let me
wear Signallers' Badges on my
arm, then nobody could see my
House Maid's knee as he calls
it.

Cus

TELEPHONE,
FLEET 67.

R. A. MESS,

EWSHOTT CAMP,

N⁹ ALDERSHOT,

HANTS.

3rd November 1929

My Dear MERRIE

    The RAT Week was a great success
I even caught one myself.   You see
as I was walking round the stables
one night to see that all was right,
and that the careless men hadn't
left too much oats in the corn bin,
I heard the corn bin making a noise
at me, and when I looked inside
there was the father and mother of
all the rats.

He tried to make out that he was
only after a few seeds for his garden
and that he was engaged on work of
National  Importance,
but I said
the running
forage account
wouldn't stand
his running away
with it, and
rang the bell for the Head Cat.   He
then told me he was a WIRKLICHGEHEIMER
REGIERUNGSRAT which means a truly
secret and confidential Rat, but that
did not save him, and I can tell you
he was a HOFSCHAUSQUEALERINAUSSER
DIENST when the Head Cat took him
away.

The Head Cat was awfully pleased
as that made his number up to one
more than the R.E. Cat.   Of course
the R.E. CAT is a Foreman of Works
and a higly technical cat, and he
has an unfair advantage, as he is
a Member of the Institute of Civil
Engineers, and can put M.I.C.E.
after his name.   Naturally if you
have got MICE after your name you
ought to be good after Rats.   Our
Head Cat is going to form a Royal
Artillery Tabby Society so that he
can put R.A.T.S after his.

Now 1 must go and practice my
Semaphorex with BILLIE.   It's very
useful for keeping the flies off in
summer, but I amke the most awful
faces in trying to send the letter
"H", as you will see from this
picture.

Your Loving "Cus"

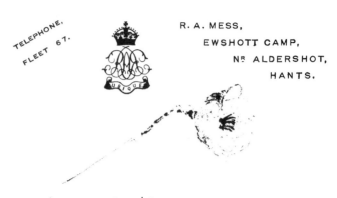

TELEPHONE,
FLEET 67.

R. A. MESS,
EWSHOTT CAMP,
Nᵣ ALDERSHOT,
HANTS.

11ᵀᴴ NOVEMBER 1929

MY DEAR BRIGHTIE

THIS IS "REMEMBRANCE
DAY", SO I TOOK SIXPENCE
OUT OF MY MONEY-BOX, AND
BOUGHT A POPPY.

OF COURSE, LIKE YOU AND MERRIE, I
WAS TOO YOUNG TO GO TO THE
GREAT WAR MYSELF BUT I'VE HEARD
ALL ABOUT IT FROM OLD "ALICE",
THE SERGEANT-MAJOR'S CHARGER. SHE'S
TWENTY-THREE, BUT YOU'D NEVER THINK
IT. IT'S THESE SHORT SKIRTS AND
BOBBED HAIR WHICH MAKES HER LOOK
SO YOUNG. I ASKED HER HOW SHE
MANAGED TO STAY ON IN THE ARMY
AND SHE TOLD ME THAT WHEN SHE
GOT TO THE OFFICIAL AGE OF
EIGHTEEN, AND OUGHT TO HAVE BEEN
PENSIONED SHE JUST KNOCKED OFF
A YEAR EACH BIRTHDAY, INSTEAD OF
ADDING ONE, AND NOW SHE'S ONLY JUST
THIRTEEN. SHE SAYS SHE'S GOING
TO STICK TO THAT NOW, AS IT'S THE
SAME NUMBER AS THE BATTERY.

WAR'S NOT ALL JAM —
EVEN PLUM AND APPLE!

TICKLER'S
PLUM
&
APPLE
JAM

AND "ALICE" TELLS US IT'S MORE
MUD THAN GLORY.

STILL IT'S OUR JOB , AND IF WE FIGHT
AGAIN I HOPE I'LL BE IN IT , AND
COME BACK WITH AS MANY MEDALS AS
ALICE . IF MY DRIVER COMES
BACK SOME DAY WITH AN EMPTY BRIDLE
I SHALL STILL BE CONTENT , FOR I
KNOW YOU'LL BUY A POPPY IN
REMEMBRANCE

OF OLD CUSTARD

R. A. MESS,

EWSHOTT CAMP,

NR ALDERSHOT,

HANTS.

16TH NOVEMBER 1929

MY DEAR MERRIE

WE DINED THE COLONEL OUT LAST NIGHT
AND THEY MADE SUCH A SCENE IN THE
UNCLE-ROOM . I CALL IT THAT BECAUSE IT COMES
BEFORE THE ANTE-ROOM. MR DAVIE WANTED
TO RIDE ME IN TO SEE THE COLONEL , BUT

HE SEEMS TO HAVE FORGOTTEN THAT HE WAS NOT

ON PARADE COMMANDING THE BATTERY , AND IN
THE MESS WE ARE ALL EQUALS. I WAS QUITE
DETERMINED TO SHOW HIM I KNEW MY MANNERS
SO I WENT OUT AND SAW THE MESS SERGEANT
AND TOLD HIM TO PUT A BOTTLE OF BURGUNDY
ON THE ICE TO DRINK THE COLONEL'S HEALTH.
IT'S VERY IMPORTANT ON YOUR FIRST APPEARANCE
AS AN HONOURABLE MEMBER TO SHOW YOU KNOW
ALL ABOUT WINE. I ONCE ORDERED A SPRING
CHICKEN AND SOME '64 PORT , BUT AS THE
WAITER HAD TO TAKE AN AXE TO CARVE THE
CHICKEN , I THINK HE MIXED UP THE DATES.
IT HAD A VERY VICTORIAN LOOK ABOUT
ITS LINGERIE , AND HAD FRILLS ROUND ITS
KNEES.

THE WAITER SAID THEY WERE MEANT TO HOLD ON BY
WHILE YOU CARVED.

THE COLONEL WAS AWFULLY AFFABLE — THERE'S NO
STAND-OFFISHNESS ABOUT HIM, AND HE GAVE ME
A CIGARETTE. DO YOU KNOW, WHEN I PICKED
UP A BOX OF MATCHES TO LIGHT IT,
IT JUMPED OUT OF MY HAND, AND

MADE A NOISE AT ME LIKE A BLUE BOTTLE
IN A PAPER BAG. I NEVER HAD SUCH

A SHOCK IN MY YOUNG LIFE, AND
WHEN I WENT TO BED I HUNG
UP MY SHOES ALL CROOKED —
LIKE THIS.

I HOPE THEY WON'T PUT IT DOWN
TO THE ICED BURGUNDY!

R.A. MESS,
EWSHOTT CAMP,
Nʀ ALDERSHOT,
HANTS.

20ᵀᴴ NOVEMBER 1929

MY DEAR MERRIE

THERE **WAS** SOMETHING WRONG WITH
THAT ICED BURGUNDY I HAD IN THE MESS
ON GUEST NIGHT. IT BROUGHT ON
MOST FRIGHTFUL DREAMS, AND I FELT AS
IF NIGHT-MARES WERE WALKING ALL OVER
ME

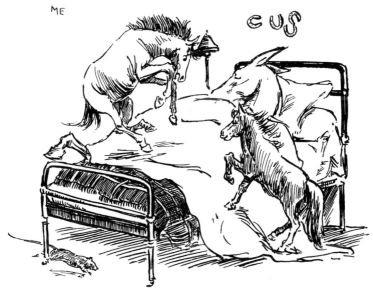

THAT LITTLE WRETCH CORA WASN'T A BIT
SYMPATHETIC , BUT JUST SAID "OH! RATS!" IN QUITE
A NASTY WAY . I'D BEEN MEANING TO COMPLAIN
ABOUT THOSE RATS MYSELF , BUT THE HEAD CAT
HAD GONE TO THE SERGEANTS' DANCE , AND I
DIDN'T LIKE DISTURBING
HIM.

WOULD YOU BELIEVE IT , CORA SAID SHE DIDN'T SEE
ANY RATS EITHER . THERE MUST BE SOMETHING
WRONG WITH HER EYES.

SHE WAS SO SNAPPY AT BREAKFAST THAT
MORNING

THAT SHE BIT THE HEAD OFF
THE PORRIDGE SPOON ! YOU SHOULD
HAVE SEEN THE COOK'S FACE. HE
TOLD CORA HER MANNERS WERE MORE
FIT FOR THE STABLE THAN THE DRAWING
ROOM, AND I THINK HE WAS QUITE
RIGHT.

HE PUT HER IN THE CORNER, AND SAID HE
WISHED TO GOODNESS SHE'D KICK THE BUCKET.
HE WASN'T A BIT PLEASED WHEN SHE
DID, FOR HE'D FORGOTTEN TO EMPTY TH
WHITE WASH OUT OF IT.

SOME PEOPLE ARE NEVER SATISFIED, BUT
I AM THANKFUL FOR SMALL MERCIES, AND
ATE HER PORRIDGE AS WELL AS MY OWN
BACON SAYS "READING MAKETH A FULL MAN"
BUT IT'S NOT HALF SO FILLING AS OUR BRAN.

EVER YOUR
CUSTARD

R.A. MESS,

EWSHOTT CAMP,

Nᴿ ALDERSHOT,

HANTS.

28ᵀᴴ NOVEMBER 1929

MY DEAR BRIGHT
 WE'VE BEEN SO BUSY ALL THIS MONTH WITH INDIVIDUAL
TRAINING THAT I DON'T KNOW HOW I'VE FOUND TIME FOR
WRITING.   YOU SEE ITS VERY IMPORTANT NOWADAYS
IN THE ARMY THAT EVERY BODY SHOULD KNOW EVERY
THING, SO WE GO TO SCHOOL IN THE AFTERNOON
AND I'M BECOMING A REGULAR "EDUCATION KATCHA"

POINTS OF THE HORSE

I'M QUITE GOOD AT READING AND WRITING,
AND I KNOW MY MULTIPLICATION TABLE UP
TO FOUR TIMES EIGHT IS FIFTY TWO, AND
ALL THAT ; BUT WHEN IT COMES TO THOSE
VULGAR FRACTIONS
I CAN'T STAND IT
BECAUSE,
AS YOU KNOW,
I HATE ANYTHING
THAT SAVOURS OF
VULGARITY.

IF ANY OF MY FRIENDS
ASKED ME TO GO FOR
A WALK WITH HIM
DRESSED LIKE THIS —
I SHOULD CUT HIM DEAD
— WITH A CHAFF-CUTTER,

I LOVE THE HISTORY
OF THE BRITISH EMPIRE
AND WROTE AN ESSAY
THE OTHER DAY ABOUT
SIR RAJAD HOWLER AND
THE BLACK HOLE OF
CALCUTTA.

AND HE'D
FIND THAT
WOULD BE
NO JOKE.

I SAID HE'D SHUT UP A HUNDRED AND
TWENTY SIX MEN IN A ROOM WITH ONE
SMALL WIDOW, AND IN THE MORNING ONLY
FIVE WERE LEFT ALIVE. I DON'T
KNOW WHY THEY ALL LAUGHED AT ME, FOR
IT'S ALL IN THE BOOK THOUGH I MAY
HAVE GOT THE NUMBERS WRONG.

YOUR LETTER AND MERRIE'S REACHED ME
TWO DAYS AGO IN HOSPITAL, AS I HAD A
SLIGHT ACCIDENT. YOU SEE I'M NOT USED
TO THESE LONG SKIRTS YET, AND MY SHOE
-MAKER WILL GIVE ME SUCH HIGH HEELS, THAT
THE FIRST TIME I WENT OUT FOR A WALK I
FAIRLY PUT MY FOOT IN IT.

THAT'S THE SECOND TIME THAT SINFUL
COBBLER'S LET ME DOWN. I'D LIKE TO

SEE HIM SCARING RATS IN THE FORE
CHAINS OF A MEDWAY BARGE AT A HALFPENNY
AN HOUR, AND FINDING HIMSELF.

SO HERE I AM
LAID UP LIKE AN
OLD GENTLEMAN WITH
THE GOUT, WHILE
BRONCHO HAS GOT
MY STAR PART
IN THE CINEMA
FILM.
STILL I'M CONSOLED
BY YOUR LETTERS
WHICH ARE VERY
REFRESHING AFTER

THE TIMES, WHICH IS DOLEFUL READING THESE
DAYS THANKS TO THE POLICY OF THE
LABOUR GOVERNMENT

YOUR LOVING

Gus.

"ST BARBARA"

R. A. MESS,
EWSHOTT CAMP,
Nᴿ ALDERSHOT,
HANTS.

4ᵀᴴ DECEMBER 1929

MY DEAR MERRIE

PERHAPS YOU DIDN'T KNOW THAT THIS IS Sᵀ BARBARA'S DAY , AND AWFULLY IMPORTANT TO US GUNNERS, AS SHE IS OUR PATRON SAINT. IT'S VERY HARD TO GET A GOOD PORTRAIT OF HER AS SHE LIVED BEFORE THE CAMERA WAS INVENTED , SO I'VE HAD TO DRAW HER FROM IMAGINATION — LIKE EVERY ONE ELSE.

I DON'T KNOW WHY SHE WAS CHOSEN AS OUR PATRON SAINT UNLESS IT WAS BECAUSE SHE WAS CANONISED . CERTAINLY THE MAN WHO WAS RESPONSIBLE FOR HER DEATH WAS STRUCK BY LIGHTENING , AND

THAT'S WHY . WE GUNNERS WEAR LIGHTENING IN OUR TIES.

IF THE MAN HADN'T BEEN BOTHERED BY LIGHTENING I DON'T KNOW WHAT WE SHOULD HAVE DONE ABOUT IT.

TODAY IS "BABS'S" BIRTHDAY — THAT'S WHY SHE WAS CALLED BARBARA — AND WE ALL CLUBBED TOGETHER TO GIVE HER A BIRTHDAY PRESENT. SHE'S GOING TO HAVE A BIG OATCAKE WITH TWELVE LUMPS OF SUGAR INSTEAD OF CANDLES STUCK IN IT. "BOBBIE" WANTED TO MAKE IT, BUT THE LAST HE MADE WASN'T A SUCCESS AND HE TOOK ALL THE HAIR OFF HIS KNEES KNEADING THE DOUGH. I CAN TELL YOU HE PUT HIS FOOT IN IT PROPERLY, AND YOU CAN SEE THE MARKS TO THIS DAY. NOW ONE HAIR IN THE SOUP MIGHT BE SWALLOWED, IF IT'S THE RIGHT KIND OF HARE, BUT WE DON'T WANT BOBBIE'S MOULTINGS IN A BIRTHDAY CAKE.

EVEN THE HARE'S BETTER IF
YOU TAKE HIS COAT OFF

BOBBIE WASN'T A BIT
PLEASED WHEN WE TOLD HIM
THAT THE BATTERY COOK
WAS TO DO THE BAKING
AND HE LOOKED ABOUT AS CONTENTED AS AN
ARMFUL OF CATS.

I'M NOT REALLY
VERY GOOD AT
DRAWING
MASSES OF CATS
BUT I DARE SAY
THEY'D LOOK AS
TANGLED AS THIS,
IF YOU TRIED TO
TRANSPORT THEM
IN LARGE NUMBERS.

ANYWAY, TO RETURN
TO "BABS'S" TEA-PARTY,
IT WAS A GREAT
SUCCESS, AND
AFTERWARDS WE
BOBBED FOR
APPLES IN THE
HORSE TROUGH.
I GOT TWO, BUT
ABEL WASN'T ABLE
TO DO IT AT ALL,

AND "BOBBIE" WAS NO GOOD AT BOBBING.
NOW THEY'RE TURNING THE LIGHTS
OUT SO I CAN'T WRITE ANY MORE

YOUR LOVING

Cus

BOBBING FOR APPLES

R A. MESS,
EWSHOTT CAMP,
Nª ALDERSHOT,
HANTS.

11ᵀᴴ DECEMBER 1929

MY DEAR BRIGHTIE

CHRISTMAS IS GETTING VERY
CLOSE AND WE ARE MAKING ALL
SORTS OF PREPARATIONS. ON
SATURDAY WE STIRRED THE PUDDING.

You KNOW THE THREE BIG BOILERS WHERE
THEY MAKE OUR BRAN MASH — WELL WE
MADE IT IN THEM , BUT "BABY" STIRRED
SO HARD THAT HE POKED THE IRON
SPOON THROUGH THE BOTTOM OF THE
BOILER , AND THE PUDDING ALL RAN OUT
THROUGH THE FIRE - PLACE.   IT WAS AN

AWFUL WASTE ,
AND WE WERE'NT
A BIT
AMUSED .

I PUT SIX PENCE OUT OF MY MONEY. BOX IN THE PUDDING I STIRRED, AND WHEN WE GOT BACK TO THE STABLE WE FOUND THAT CORA HAD LEFT ONE OF HER SHOES BEHIND. THE LITTLE WRETCH HAD BEEN STIRRING THE PUDDING WITH HER HAND, AND IT WAS SO STICKY THAT THE SHOE GOT LEFT BEHIND. CORA SAYS IT WILL BE GOOD LUCK FOR WHOEVER FINDS IT — BUT THAT'S THE SORT OF LUCK I CAN DO WITHOUT.

I THINK IT'S AN AWFUL SHAME THAT NONE OF US MULES HAVE STOCKINGS TO HANG UP ON CHRISTMAS EVE. NEARLY ALL THE PONIES IN THE BATTERY HAVE WHITE STOCKINGS, OR SOCKS AND THEY ARE HORRIDLY STUCK UP ABOUT IT.

I SHALL BE ALL RIGHT THIS YEAR BECAUSE

"STOCKINGS", WHO IS A GREAT FRIEND OF MINE, HAS TWO PAIRS, AND HAS PROMISED TO LEND ME ONE.

YOUR LOVING

CUS

R. A. MESS,

EWSHOTT CAMP,

Nᴿ ALDERSHOT,

HANTS.

20ᵀᴴ DECEMBER 1929.

Y DEAR MERRIE
ᴬᴺᴰ BRIGHT

I HEAR YOU ARE GOING AWAY FOR
CHRISTMAS SO I'M WRITING NOW
TO WISH YOU BOTH A VERY MERRY
ONE, AND A BRIGHT NEW YEAR.
I HOPE YOU'LL HAVE A
LOVELY CHRISTMAS TREE
WITH LOTS OF CARROTS
AND ALL THE THINGS
SUPERIOR PEOPLE LIKE,
SUCH AS LUMPS OF
SUGAR, AND APPLES.
YOU'VE GOT TO BE
CAREFUL OF THE APPLES
NOWADAYS, BECAUSE
THEY MAKE SOAP ONES
SO LIKE THE REAL THING
THAT YOU MAY MAKE THE
SAME MISTAKE AS 'BOBBIE' DID LAST YEAR.

HE MADE AN AWFUL FACE WHEN HE FOUND OUT, AND WE ALL LAUGHED AT HIM AND SAID IT SERVED HIM RIGHT, AS HE HADN'T BRUSHED HIS TEETH THAT MORNING. WE HAD A SUGAR MOUSE WITH A WOOLLY TAIL FOR THE HEAD CAT, AND HE WAS ENORMOUSLY PLEASED TO BE REMEMBERED. HE SAID HE'D KEEP IT TO SUGAR HIS "GUN FIRE TEA" WHEN HE'D HAD A LATE NIGHT OUT AFTER THE RATS.

HE LOOKS LIKE NOTHING ON EARTH WHEN HE COMES IN IN THE MORNING, BUT HE FEELS MUCH BETTER IF

HE HAS MICE IN HIS TEA LIKE "ALICE THROUGH THE LOOKING GLASS".*

I'LL SEND YOU EACH ONE OF THE BATTERY CHRISTMAS CARDS . I REALLY DON'T THINK THEM VERY FUNNY BECAUSE THE MAJOR DOESN'T DRAW MULES AS WELL AS I DO . I EXPECT HE HAS MORE EXPERIENCE OF DONKEYS AT MARGATE.

HE HASN'T THE RIGHT FEELING FOR A MULE SOMEHOW, AND THE EXPRESSIONS HE GIVES US ARE SIMPLY AWFUL . I CAN'T REPEAT THEM.

* HE SAYS "CATS IN THE COFFEE" WAS A MISTAKE OF LEWIS CAROL'S , WHO WAS MISLED BY THE ALITERATION (WHATEVER THAT MAY BE) : OF COURSE IT OUGHT TO HAVE BEEN "PUT . RATS IN THE COFFEE AND MICE IN THE TEA". THAT MAKES SENSE.

75

If I DIDN'T THINK I'D FRIGHTEN YOU GETTING ON MY HIND LEGS I'D LOVE TO PULL A CRACKER WITH YOU ON CHRISTMAS DAY, BUT AS I HEAR YOU ARE GOING AWAY YOU MUST TAKE THE WORD FOR THE DEED, AND ACCEPT THE HEARTIEST CHRISTMAS WISHES OF

YOUR OLD

CUS.

R. A. MESS,

EWSHOTT CAMP,

Nᴿ ALDERSHOT,

HANTS.

26ᵀᴴ DECEMBER 1929

MY DEAR MERRIE & BRIGHT

THANK YOU EVER SO MUCH FOR YOUR LOVELY CHRISTMAS CARDS WHICH ARE SO MUCH ADMIRED THAT I'VE HAD TO TAKE THEM DOWN FROM THE STABLE WALL AND PUT THEM IN THE BATTERY OFFICE FOR SAFE CUSTODY. I COULDN'T KEEP THE OTHER MULES OUT OF MY STALL, AND THEY ALL ASKED IF IT WAS THE ITALIAN PICTURES WHICH HAD JUST COME OVER IN THE "DAINTY ALLIGATOR" OR THE "LEONARDO DA WHISKY".

I SAID THERE WAS NOTHING ITALIAN ABOUT THEM , AND
THEY WERE THE ENGLISH SCHOOL , A LONG WAY
AFTER LANDSEER . CORA ACTUALLY DIDN'T
KNOW WHO LANDSEER WAS So I TOLD HER
HE WAS THE MAN WHO PUT THE LIONS IN
TRAFALGAR SQUARE TO KEEP NELSON FROM
COMING DOWN FROM HIS COLUMN . THEY'RE
SUCH FRIGHTFUL LIONS THAT I DON'T WONDER
HE KEEPS OUT OF THE WAY , AND DOESN'T

LIKE BEING ASSOCIATED WITH THEM. ALL THE BEST
LIONS CURL UP THEIR PAWS WHEN THEY LIE DOWN
BUT THESE CAN'T BE THE MOST EXPENSIVE KIND
FOR THEY KEEP THEM STRAIGHT OUT LIKE A
SPHYNX. THAT IS A MYTHICAL ANIMAL , NOW
EXTINCT , BUT FOUND ON THE CAP BADGES OF SOME
INFANTRY REGIMENTS .

CORA WAS SO MUCH TAKEN WITH THE HAY STACKS IN YOUR PICTURES THAT SHE WANTED TO TASTE THEM. I WISH YOU'D SEND HER A DRAWING OF A THISTLE TO SHOW WHAT A LITTLE DONKEY SHE IS. AS LONG AS I HAD THEM UP I COULDN'T KEEP THE PLACE TO MYSELF, AND EVERYBODY JOSTLED IN TO SEE THEM TILL THERE WASN'T ROOM TO SWING A CAT.

WHY PEOPLE WANT TO SWING CATS, OR TO USE THEM AT ALL AS AN INSTRUMENT OF MENSURATION, IS BEYOND MY COMPREHENSION. I KNOW THEY HATE IT AND ALWAYS TRY TO GET OUT. THE HEAD CAT SAYS THE ONLY SWINGING HE DOES IS SWINGING THE LEAD WHEN HE COMES UP TO THE OFFICE.

IT WAS VERY NICE OF YOU BOTH TO COME AND SEE ME ON SUNDAY, BUT I WISH YOU'D SWUM YOUR DUCKS IN MY WATER TROUGH INSTEAD OF THE RIGHT SECTION ONE. I NEVER SAW A DUCK LIKE YOURS BEFORE AND DID WANT TO SEE HIM SWIM. WE HAVEN'T A DUCK IN THE BATTERY BUT THERE IS OLD "DRAKE" IN D SUBSECTION WHO ISN'T NEARLY AS HIGHLY COLOURED AS YOURS.

THANK YOU AGAIN FOR THE CHRISTMAS
CARDS

YOUR OLD
CUS

R. A. MESS,

EWSHOTT CAMP,

Nᴿ ALDERSHOT,

HANTS.

31ˢᵗ DECEMBER 1929

My DEAR BRIGHT

A VERY HAPPY NEW YEAR
TO YOU AND MERRIE, AND MAY
YOU HAVE MANY MORE OF THEM.

I WISH IT HAD BEEN NICE AND
SNOWY AS THEN WE COULD HAVE
GONE OUT IN THE WOODS AND HAVE
BROUGHT IN THE MULE LOG. OF
COURSE IF YOU DRAG IT IN, IT'S CALLED
A YULE LOG, BUT IF I PULL IT
IT'S A MULE ONE

I'M NOT GOING TO MAKE ANY GOOD RESOLUTIONS

THIS YEAR AS I ALWAYS FORGET THEM. LAST

YEAR I WAS GOING TO THE SALES TO BUY
A CAMI-SHIMMIE OR A BOLERO OR
SOMETHING LIKE THAT , AND WHILE I
WAS WONDERING WHETHER I'D HAVE KASHA
OR KIA ORA I STEPPED ON THE STAIR
CASE WHILE WAS GOING UP INSTEAD
OF DOWN . I MUST HAVE MADE
TWENTY RESOLUTIONS A MINUTE BEFORE
I GOT TO THE BOTTOM , AND THEN I
MADE ONE I'VE KEPT EVER SINCE —

NEVER TO GO BY TUBE AGAIN. AS A MATTER OF FACT THE TRAFFIC IN THE STREETS THESE DAYS IS SIMPLY AWFUL, AND UNLESS YOU ARE PRETTY NIPPY YOU'VE NO MORE CHANCE THAN A DOG WITH TALLOW LEGS CHASING AN ASBESTOS CAT ACROSS THE SAHARA.

IN FACT, NOWADAYS, THE PEOPLE WHO DON'T USE MOTORS MAY BE DIVIDED INTO THE QUICK AND THE DEAD.

I'M FAIRLY QUICK AT SEEING JOKES AND I LAUGHED THE FIRST TIME THAT I HEARD THAT ONE.

DID YOU EVER SEE A MULE LAUGH? WELL WHEN HE (OR SHE) DOES HE (OR SHE) WRINKLES UP HIS (OR HER) NOSE LIKE THIS

P. T. O

YOUR LAUGHING

CUS

R. A. MESS,
EWSHOTT CAMP,
Nʳ ALDERSHOT,
HANTS.

19ᵗʰ JANUARY 1930.

MY DEAR BRIGHT

AFTER YOU LEFT TODAY I SLIPPED OVER TO THE MESS AND GOT SOME NOTEPAPER. I'D COMPLETELY RUN OUT, AND LAST TIME YOU CAME HERE Mʳ DAVEY WOULN'T LET ME GO OVER TO THE MESS. I THINK I PUNISHED HIM THOUGH FOR I ATE A ROW OF CURLY CABBAGES AS A SALAD, AND I SAW HIM CHASING THE COWS WITH A PACKET OF INSECT POWDER SHOUTING THAT HE HOPED THEIR RABBIT WOULD DIE.

I DON'T THINK THEY MIND A BIT AND I DOUBT IF THEY EVEN KEEP A GUINEA PIG. THEY CERTAINLY CAN'T KEEP OUT OF THE MESS GARDEN.

I DID ENJOY GOING FOR A RIDE WITH YOU THIS MORNING AND DIDN'T WANT TO GO BACK TO THAT DULL STABLE A BIT. YOU SEE WE ALL HAD TO GO OUT TO WATER IN FIVE MINUTES, SO I MIGHT JUST AS WELL HAVE STAYED OUTSIDE. IF YOU HADN'T ENTICED ME WITH THAT SUGAR, I'D HAVE BEEN THERE YET

I REMEMBER WHEN WE EMBARKED TO COME
TO ENGLAND THERE WERE TWO MULES
WHO JUST WOULDN'T WALK ON TO THE
SHIP

AND WHILE THEY WERE ALL TUGGING
AND HAULING AT THEM , A PADRE
CAME UP AND ASKED IF HE
COULD HELP. THE SERGEANT IN
CHARGE SAID PERHAPS HE COULD
TELL HIM HOW NOAH MANAGED TO
GET THE TWO MULES INTO THE
ARK.

I THINK THE DONKEY HAD SOMETHING
TO DO WITH IT , BUT THAT'S ANOTHER
STORY , AS MR KIPLING TELLS US.

R. A. MESS,

EWSHOTT CAMP,

Nᴿ ALDERSHOT,

HANTS.

25ᵀᴴ JANUARY 1930

MY DEAR BRIGHT

I'M FEELING RATHER PART-WORN

THIS MORNING , WHICH MEANS

NEARLY WORN OUT , AFTER

A VERY LATE NIGHT IN

THE MESS .

I DIDN'T FANCY MY

BREAKFAST PORRIDGE

A BIT !

I SAW "BROWNIE" THIS AFTERNOON AND
TOLD HER SHE WAS QUITE OLD
ENOUGH TO
BECOME
A
GIRL GUIDE
LIKE

SUGAR-
YOUR LOVING

CUS

THE BRAN THEY GIVE US NOW IS A
DISGRACE . IT HAS NO BODY IN
IT LIKE THE KIND THEY USED TO
STUFF THE BODIES OF DOLLS WITH
WHEN I

WAS
QUITE A
YOUNG
GIRL.

NOW THAT
I'M OLDER,
I THINK
I LIKE
BRANDY
BETTER.

ONLY IT
DOESN'T
LIKE ME 
AND FEELS LIKE A TORCHLIGHT PROCESSION

GOING DOWN MY THROAT. I SOME-
TIMES WISH I HAD A NECK LIKE
A GIRAFFE OR AN OSTRICH ; THEN
I SHOULD BE ABLE TO TASTE IT
ALL THE WAY DOWN .

I WOULD'T LIKE TO
COME OUT IN SPOTS LIKE
THE BEAST I HAVE
DRAWN , BECAUSE THEY
MIGHT THINK IT WAS
SOMETHING CATCHING , AND
SEND ME TO HOSPITAL .
IT WAS RAINING
VERY HARD LAST NIGHT
AND I WAS AFRAID
I SHOULN'T BE ABLE
TO GO OVER

TO THE

MESS , BECAUSE
MY FEET MIGHT
GET MUDDY
AND MAKE A
MESS OF THE
CARPET , BUT

MR DAVEY WAS VERY . KIND , AND PUT
ON MY GOLOSHES , SO WITH THEM
AND AN OLD RUG I KEPT AS DRY AS
A BONE OUT SIDE .

INSIDE WAS QUITE ANOTHER MATTER, AND
I DON'T MIND TELLING YOU (IN CONFIDENCE)
THAT I HAD TO HELP HIM HOME
AFTERWARDS

YOURS TO A CINDER

CUS

R.A. MESS,
EWSHOTT CAMP,
Nᴿ ALDERSHOT,
HANTS.

31ˢᵗ JANUARY 1930.

MY DEAR BRIGHT

I WAS TREMENDOUSLY

BUCKED UP

TO GET YOUR

LETTER

THIS MORNING

THAT

I

DIDN'T

KNOW

WHETHER

I WAS

ON

MY HEAD

OR MY HEELS .   I SIMPLY LEAPED

OUT OF BED TO READ IT , AND

MADE CORA JEALOUS , AND MY BREAKFAST

COLD.

CUSTARD

93

IF YOU'RE ONLY SIX AND CAN DO THE MULTIPLICATION TABLE UP TO SIX TIMES , I OUGHT TO BE ABLE TO DO IT UP TO TWELVE TIMES AS I'M NEARLY TWELVE . BUT I CAN'T AND I'M THINKING OF BUYING A RABBIT TO HELP ME , AS I HEAR THEY MULTIPLY SO RAPIDLY.

I TOLD MR DAYEY BUT HE SAID HIS HEART WAS FAIR SCALDED WITH THOSE SAME RABBITS WHO HAD ATE UP ALL THE PINKS AND WALL FLOWERS ON HIM , AND HE WISHED OLD NICK WOULD SWEEP HADES WITH THEM, AND BURN THE BROOM AFTER . I SUPPOSE "OLD NICK" IS MR NICHOLSON , WHO'S GONE TO INDIA , WHERE IT'S HOT , BUT I DON'T KNOW WHERE HADES IS , UNLESS ITS THE OLD

RATION STORE, WHERE THERE WAS A LITTER OF YOUNG CATS LITERALLY MIXED UP WITH THE BREAD.

I CAN TELL YOU, THERE WAS NEARLY A CAT-ASTROPHE, WHEN THE OLD COLONEL CAME IN AND FOUND THEM, AND THE LAST HEAD CAT BUT ONE LOST HIS JOB.

I BELIEVE IN THE END HE WENT TO THE VOCATIONAL TRAINING CENTRE TO LEARN HOW TO MAKE MOUSE TRAPS WHICH IS THE ONLY WAY HE IS LIKELY TO CATCH ANY MICE.

I'M AFRAID HE WAS A LOAFER, OTHERWISE HE'D

NEVER HAVE WANTED TO LIVE IN THE BREAD STORE.

Now I MUST MAKE UP THE FORAGE ACCOUNT FOR THE MONTH AND SEE IF I CAN SCROUNGE AN ENVELOPE FROM THE BATTERY OFFICE FOR THIS.

YOURS EVER

Gus

R. A. MESS,

EWSHOTT CAMP,

Nᴿ ALDERSHOT,

HANTS.

14ᵀᴴ FEBRUARY 1930

MY DEAR MERRIE

I FIND, ON LOOKING THROUGH MY LETTER BOOK, THAT YOU ARE QUITE RIGHT (AS LADIES ALWAYS ARE) AND THAT BRIGHT HAS HAD THE LAST TWO, IF NOT THREE, OF MY MISSIVES. .

THIS IS ALL WRONG, AND I SHALL GIVE THE
BATTERY CLERK WHAT FOR - WITH THE CHILL
OFF, IF IT HAPPENS AGAIN. I WOULD
HAVE ANSWERED YOUR LETTER LONG AGO, BUT
ONLY GOT IT THIS MORNING. AS IT WAS
ADDRESSED C/O OF THE MAJOR WHO HAS
BEEN AWAY IN AN AEROPLANE SINCE SUNDAY.
HE FLAPPED OVER HERE IN AN "ATLAS"

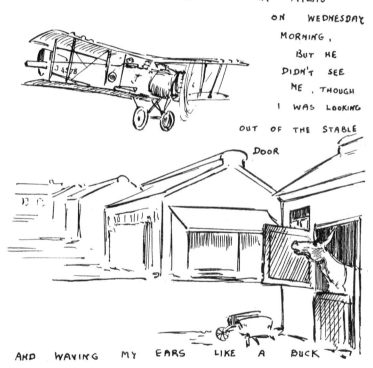

ON WEDNESDAY
MORNING,
BUT HE
DIDN'T SEE
ME, THOUGH
I WAS LOOKING
OUT OF THE STABLE
DOOR

AND WAVING MY EARS LIKE A BUCK

RABBIT.

OF COURSE THE CLOUDS WERE VERY LOW THAT MORNING, BUT AS I'M NEARLY THE ONLY YELLOW MULE IN THE BRIGADE I THINK HE MIGHT HAVE RETURNED MY SALUTE. I EXPECT HE WAS FEELING A BIT "LOOPY" BEING SO HIGH UP FOR THE FIRST TIME. IT WAS THE NEAREST TO HEAVEN HE'S GOT YET, AND HE SAYS THERE'S A DRAUGHT UP THERE THAT WOULD DRAW A YOUNG CAT UP.

I'M SO SORRY TO HEAR THAT YOU AND BRIGHTIE HAVE BOTH BEEN CHILLY, BUT BELIEVE ME, ON SUCH OCCASIONS "BED'S THE BEST". I EAT MINE, WHEN I HAVE NOTHING BETTER TO DO, SO I OUGHT TO KNOW. OAT STRAWS THE BEST, AS IT'S NOT SO PRICKLY AS WHEAT AND WE ALWAYS ASK FOR IT.

I OUGHT REALLY TO HAVE SENT YOU
A VALENTINE , BUT THEY DON'T HAVE
VERY GOOD ONES NOWADAYS. I
REMEMBER THE ONES WITH WHISKERS ALL
ROUND LIKE THE LACE ON MY WHAT
-DO-YOU CALL 'EMS

SOMETHING LIKE THIS , ONLY MORE SO.

YOUR LOVING

Cus

R. A. MESS,

EWSHOTT CAMP,

Nʳ ALDERSHOT,

HANTS.

16ᵀᴴ FEBRUARY 1930

My DEAR BRIGHTIE

THAT RHYMES WITH "NIGHTIE"
DOESN'T IT?, WHICH REMINDS ME
THAT I AM VERY SORRY TO HEAR
YOU'RE IN BED AGAIN, SNEEZING

LIKE A HOURI WITH HAY FEVER.
I ALWAYS MIX UP HOURIS WITH
HARPIES, BUT I KNOW ONE IS NICER

THAN THE OTHER , THOUGH THE HARPIES
DON'T CARRY HARPS , AND THEIR WINGS
ARE THE ONLY ANGELIC PART ABOUT
THEM. I THINK THEY'RE PRETTY
EXTINCT NOW THAT THE MILITANT SUF-
-FRAGETTES HAVE DIED OUT
AND YOU'LL ONLY FIND THEM
IN A MUSEUM
WITH THE DODO -
WHO LOOKED RATHER
LIKE THIS - BUT MORE
SO , IF POSSIBLE.

I DO HOPE YOU
HAVEN'T GOT
"PSITTACOSIS" , (WHICH
IS A VERY SNEEZY
-SOUNDING COMPLAINT)
AND I DON'T KNOW
WHAT I'D DO IF YOU TURNED INTO A
PARROT AND STARTED GRIMPING UP
MY TAIL UTTERING HORRID IMPLICATIONS!
I DON'T MIND A PAIR OF LOVE
BIRDS LIKE YOU AND MERRIE ABOUT
THE STABLE , BUT I'D GET AS
KICKSOME AS CORA IF A RED
AND BLUE MACAW STARTED MONKEYING
WITH MY TAIL

I WOULDN'T MIND SO MUCH IF YOU
TURNED INTO A PIERRETTE
OR EVEN
A PENGUIN
LIKE

"SQUEAK"

THOUGH HER
FIGURE'S A BIT
DOWDY ACCORDING
TO 1930 STANDARDS.
BUT
ON THE WHOLE

I'D MUCH SOONER

HAVE YOU JUST AS YOU ARE

So STOP THIS SNEEZING ENTERTAINMENT,

AND COME AND SEE YOUR OLD

FRIEND

Cus

R. A. MESS,

EWSHOTT CAMP,

Nᴿ ALDERSHOT,

HANTS.

TELEPHONE,
FLEET 67.

2ᴺᴰ MARCH 1930

MY DEAR MERRIE

I WAS CHEERED UP AT SEEING YOU BOTH THIS MORNING FOR I'VE HAD A VERY DULL WEEK, AND WASN'T EVEN INVITED INTO THE MESS ON GUEST NIGHT TO SAY GOODBYE TO JASPAR. IT'S A HARD WORLD FOR US WOMEN, AS EVEN HAZEL WASN'T ALLOWED IN. I GOT NO SYMPATHY OUT OF THE HEAD CAT WHO TELLS ME HE'S GOT A SEMI-DETACHED WIFE AT CRONDAL WHO TEACHES IN A SUNDAY SCHOOL AND NEVER GOES TO THE MOVIES.

WHEN   JASPER   GETS   AMONG   ALL   THOSE
CAMELS   AND   BYLES   I'M   AFRAID
HE'LL   FORGET   US   KATCHAS,   AND
DREAM   ABOUT   NOTHING   BUT
GREAT   BIG

BEARS

AND

TIGERS

AND THINGS THAT GO BUMP IN THE NIGHT. DO YOU KNOW I THINK I SHALL HAVE TO TAKE TO WEARING SPECTACLES ALTOGETHER, FOR TODAY I MISTOOK BRIGHTIE'S FINGER FOR A CARROT !

IT WAS SO SMALL AND JUICY THAT I DID NOT REALISE MY MISTAKE TILL I'D TASTED IT, AND POOR BRIGHT WAS HOPPING LIKE A HERRING ON THE GRIDDLE.

I REALLY OUGHT TO WRITE TO HER TO EXPLAIN BUT SECTION TRAINING BEGINS ON TUESDAY AFTER WE HAVE ALL HAD A DENTAL INSPECTION.

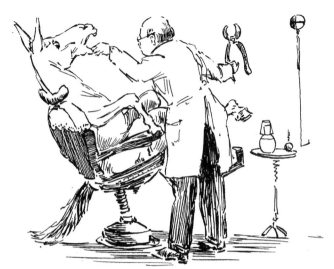

I HATE GOING TO THE DENTIST . IT GIVES
ME POSITIVE PAIN ! NOBODY LOVES
THEM , AND WHEN CORA OVERSLEEPS
IN THE MORNING WE TELL HER THAT
SHE LIES LIKE A TOOTH-DRAWER.

NOW NO MORE TILL EASTER
WHEN WE GET OUR NEXT HOLIDAY

LOVE TO BRIGHTIE

from her contrite

Cus.

R. A. MESS,
EWSHOTT CAMP,
Nᴿ ALDERSHOT,
HANTS.

MY DEAR BRIGHT

LIKE YOU I AM ENJOYING
A LITTLE "OTIUM CUM DIGGIN
A 'TATY' IN THE MESS GARDEN
(WHEN Mᴿ DAVEY DOESN'T
CATCH ME AT IT)

SINCE THOSE VERY WET NIGHTS

109

ON MANOEUVRES I HAVE BEEN
RESTING MY LEG

AND I'M SORRY TO SAY I
DID NOT GET DOWN TO CHURCH
LAST SUNDAY. I WANTED
TO GO TO THE ODIHAM
SHOW WITH "STOCKINGS"
WHO WAS JUMPING, BUT

WAS AFRAID I WOULD MAKE
MY OTHER KNEE MATCH THE
OTHER ONE WHICH HAS NEVER
RECOVERED SINCE LAST LENT

I REALLY MUST COMPLAIN TO
THAT PADRE ABOUT THE SIZE
OF THE FOOT STOOLS IN HIS
CHURCH . THEY ARE ALL VERY
WELL FOR YOU AND MERRIE
BUT THEY GIVE ME HOUSE
MAID'S KNEE , AND MAKE
ME WANT TO
"CUSS"

R. A. MESS,
EWSHOTT CAMP,
Nʳ ALDERSHOT,
HANTS.

APRIL 1930

MY DEAR MERRIE AND BRIGHT

I'M SO GLAD THAT LENT IS NEARLY OVER, AND THE EASTER HOLIDAYS HAVE BEGUN.

WE STOPPED TRAINING ON THURSDAY FOR FIVE DAYS, AND I NIPPED OVER TO ALDERSHOT IN THE AFTERNOON TO BUY SOME

EASTER EGGS.

I HOPE THESE RABBITS WILL
REMIND YOU OF ME , AS THERE
IS A SORT OF SIMILARITY ABOUT
THE EARS , AND I THINK
THE CARROT
IS A GOOD
TOUCH TOO
  WE HAVE BEEN
HAVING THEM FOR
A TREAT ON
SUNDAYS (WHICH IS'NT
A FAST DAY IN LENT)
So THE PADRE HAS NO
OBJECTION TO OUR EATING THEM,
AND MR DAVEY SAYS THEY
MAKE OUR EYES BRIGHT. MINE
POSITIVELY GLISTEN WHEN I
SEE THEM COMING.
    I'M SO SORRY YOU BOTH
GOT MEASLES , AND COULD'NT
COME TO SEE ME, FOR SO LONG.
THE MAJOR IS So FUSSY AND

WAS AFRAID OF THE SHOW MULES
COMING OUT IN SPOTS , AS
THEY DID YEAR BEFORE LAST.

WE HAD A GUEST NIGHT ABOUT
A WEEK AGO
AND INVITED
ALL THE
DOCTORS
UP FROM
CROOKHAM
CAMP.

OF COURSE
I WAS THERE
AND DIDN'T
GO HOME
TILL MORNING.

I WAS HAVING MY BREAKFAST
IN BED , WHEN THEY TOLD ME
A POLICEMAN WANTED TO SEE
ME AND MR DAVEY. I ONLY
HAD TIME TO SLIP A RUG ON
OVER MY NIGHTIE WHEN HE
CAME IN , AND SAID THE'RE'D

BEEN A BURGLARY, AND SOMEBODY
HAD TAKEN 14 BATTERY'S SAFE.
    HE WANTED TO KNOW IF WE'D
DONE IT FOR A JOKE!
FANCY ME BURGLING FOR
FUN. I TOLD HIM
TO GO AND SEE
IF THE HEAD CAT
WAS A CAT
BURGLAR, BUT
HE WASN'T A
BIT AMUSED.

    A VERY HAPPY EASTER
    TO YOU BOTH

        YOUR LOVING

            GUS.

R. A. MESS,
EWSHOTT CAMP,
Nᴿ ALDERSHOT,
HANTS.

10ᵀᴴ MAY 1930

My DEAR BRIGHT

THANK YOU VERY MUCH
FOR YOUR LETTER , WHICH
QUITE CHEERED ME UP , AS I
WAS FEELING RATHER SORE ON
TWO POINTS

ONE IN THE MIDDLE OF THE
BACK — WHERE "CHERRY" BIT
ME YESTERDAY (I ONLY ASKED
HER
IF
SHE
LIKED
CARROTS
AND
SHE
MADE
A RUDE
REMARK ABOUT DONKEYS AND

116

THISTLES, SO I KICKED HER SHINS WELL FOR HER.

THE OTHER IS THAT THEY'VE TAKEN ME OFF SIGNALLING, AND MADE ME CARRY THE GREAT COATS SO NOW, I LOOK LIKE AN OLD CLOTHES MAN

OR AN UMPIRE AT A CRICKET MATCH.

I WAS WALKING ROUND THOSE
TWO BRASS GUNS OUTSIDE THE
GUARD ROOM LAST SUNDAY TO
SEE WHETHER THE CLOVER THAT
GROWS THERE, COULD HAVE BEEN
MISTAKEN BY Mr DAVEY FOR SHAMROCK
EXCEPT AFTER A LATE GUEST
NIGHT,
WHEN I HEARD
A GREAT
COMMOTION
IN ONE OF
THE GUNS
AND
FOUND.
THAT
A
TOM-TIT
HAD BUILT HIS NEST IN IT WITHOUT ASKING
THE BARRACK WARDEN. OF COURSE
IT HAD TO BE REPORTED IN THE
"WEEKLY INCREASE OF MARRIED FAMILIES"
AND I EXPECT NEXT TIME I GO
LOOKING FOR FOUR-LEAVED CLOVER
I SHALL FIND A BLACK AND
WHITE NOTICE PUT UP BY THE

SAPPERS
SOMETHING
LIKE THIS.

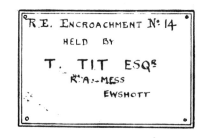

R.E. ENCROACHMENT N° 14
HELD BY
T. TIT ESQ⁸
R.A.-MESS
EWSHOTT

THE OATS ARE NONE SO BAD
THESE HARD TIMES, AND I GET
AS MANY AS I CAN BY EATING
"CROKE'S" WHILE HE IS ARGUING
WITH "CORA" ABOUT THE
LENGTH OF HER SKIRT FOR
ASCOT. I'VE MADE UP
MY MIND TO HAVE MINE LONG,
ANY WAY, AS I'VE HAD QUITE
ENOUGH OF SHOWING MY KNEES.

YOUR LOVING, BUT
DISCUSTED
CUS.

I ASK
YOU
IS THIS
A
PROPER
LOAD

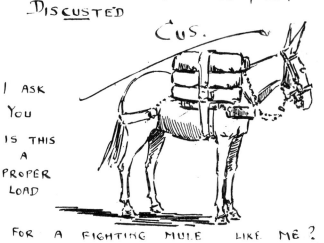

FOR A FIGHTING MULE LIKE ME?

R. A. MESS,

EWSHOTT CAMP,

Nᴿ ALDERSHOT,

HANTS.

20ᵀᴴ JUNE 1930

MY DEAR MERRIE & BRIGHT

I'VE JUST SEEN THE
PHOTOGRAPHS THE MAJOR TOOK OF
US ALL ON WEDNESDAY AFTERNOON
AND I MUST SAY I DON'T THINK
HE HAS DONE US JUSTICE. HE
MIGHT HAVE KNOWN THAT GREEN
HEDGE WOULDN'T SUIT MY COMPLEXION,
AND HE WOULD'NT LET ME PUT ON
MY LONG ASCOT FROCK TO HIDE
MY KNEES.

I SHOULD
HAVE
LOOKED
GRAND IN
MY FLOWERED
ORGANDIE
WITH A
BUNCH OF
ASPIDISTRAS
CAUGHT IN AT
THE WAIST.

I DO LIKE THE PICTURE OF YOU TWO
WITH BRIGHT PLAYING THE KETTLEDRUMS.

BUT I THINK IT OUGHT
TO HAVE BEEN TAKEN
LIKE THIS, WITH
MORE LIFE ABOUT
IT.

I'M AFRAID
BRIGHT MOVED
THE CAMERA IN
THE ONE SHE TOOK,
FOR SHE HARDLY
CAUGHT US AT ALL,
AND HAS GIVEN MR
DAVEY A DOUBLE SET
OF BUTTONS AND TWO
FACES. IT'S RATHER FLATTERING OF
MY RIGHT KNEE THOUGH.

I HAD AN AWFUL TIME AT
ASCOT YESTERDAY, AND THE ONLY
RACE I RAN IN WAS THE

GRAND STAND CUP WHEN IT BEGAN
TO RAIN.

A GREAT LUMP OF THUNDER ROLLED
AFTER ME , AND I LOST HALF OF MY
NEW SKIRT IN THE MUD . THAT
UNFEELING BRUTE CROKE ATE THE
OTHER HALF IN THE NIGHT , WHEN
I'D HUNG IT OUT TO DRY ON
THE RALE . NO MORE RACING
FOR ME THIS YEAR .

YOUR LOVING

GUS

R.A. MESS,

EWSHOTT CAMP,

Nᵣ ALDERSHOT,

HANTS,

UBIQUE

JULY 2ᴺᴰ

EXIT TO
RING Nᵒ1

MY DEAR BRIGHTIE

You OUGHT TO HAVE BEEN AT THE HORSE SHOW ON WEDNESDAY AND THURSDAY TO SEE US MULES COLLECTING THE PRIZES. WE GOT TWO RED ROSETTES, A BLUE, AND A PINK ONE. I BATTERY GOT TWO GREEKS, AND 14 A BLUE — AND THAT'S ALL THERE WERE, SO WE DIDN'T LEAVE ANYTHING FOR ANYBODY ELSE.

I REALLY THINK IF I'D ENTERED I'D HAVE GOT SOMETHING FOR THE FIRST PRIZE WAS TAKEN BY THAT OLD WITCH "DELLA". SHE HAD IT THREE YEARS AGO, BUT EVER SINCE SHE'S GOT SO LAZY THAT SHE BLACKS HER LEGS, SOONER THAN MEND THE HOLES IN HER STOCKINGS.

123

SHE ACTUALLY WENT
TO THE SHOW THIS
YEAR WITH A PAIR
THAT WERE MORE
HOLEY THAN RIGHTEOUS,
AND I SAW MR DAVEY
TRYING TO REPAIR THE
DAMAGE WITH A PAINT
POT. I DON'T HOLD
WITH ALL THIS 'MAKING UP'
IN PUBLIC, SO I TURNED
MY HEAD THE OTHER WAY
STILL IT WAS PRETTY
CUNNING OF THE OLD CAT TO GET A GENTLEMAN TO
UNDERTAKE HER RUNNING REPAIRS.

I WENT OVER TO THE OFFICERS'
MESS ON WEDNESDAY NIGHT
JUST TO CONGRATULATE THEM
ON OUR WINNING THE
CHALLENGE SHIELD

FOR THE THIRD TIME, BUT BEFORE   I COULD GET IN

TO DRINK THE HEALTH OF THE TEAM THE PADRE
(WHO WAS DINING THERE) ASKED ME WHY I WASN'T AT
SUNDAY SCHOOL LAST WEEK. I COULDN'T THINK OF
A REASON SO I ASKED HIM WHY HE WASN'T AT
THE SHOW TODAY. AS HE SAID HE WAS
TOO BUSY I DESCRIBED IT ALL FOR HIM, BUT
HE WAS NO GOOD AT THE "ACTIVITY RIDE".
I DID CATCH HIM FIRST BOUNCE, BUT AT
THE SECOND HE WENT FOR SIX, AND WAS
FIELDED BY THE ADJUTANT ON THE BOUNDARY.
I HAD A GREAT EVENING IN THE MESS
AFTER THAT, BUT IT WOULD TAKE A
HANDY HUNTER TO FIND
HIS WAY OUT
OF THAT
MESS AFTER A
GUEST NIGHT
AND WHEN I
GOT TO MY
STABLE I
FOUND I HAD
A CORKSCREW
IN MY HAND
INSTEAD OF
MY LATCH-KEY.
THERE WAS SUCH A FUNNY
ACCOUNT OF THE SHOW NEXT DAY
IN THE MORNING POST IN WHICH THEY
SAID THAT WE WON IT WITH A TRULY

MAGNIFICENT TEAM OF RED "AUSTRALIAN CANARIES". I'VE HEARD MULES CALLED SOME FUNNY THINGS IN MY TIME, BUT NEVER THAT, AND I CAN'T FIND THE EXPRESSION IN THE "INSIDE COMPLETE YOU ARE BRITTANIAWARE", BREWER'S DICTIONARY OF PHRASE AND FABLE, OR ANYWHERE ELSE.

CONSEQUENTLY, I HESITATE TO SUBSCRIBE MYSELF

YOUR YELLOW AUSTRALIAN CANARY

CUS

TELEPHONE,
FLEET 67.

R. A. MESS,
EWSHOTT CAMP,
Nᴮ ALDERSHOT,
HANTS.

Cᵀᴴ SEPTEMBER 1930

MY DEAR CARRIE

MANY, MANY HAPPY RETURNS OF THE DAY. I DO THINK YOU WERE CLEVER TO ARRANGE TO HAVE YOUR BIRTHDAY IN SEPTEMBER, SO THAT YOU COULD START ON OYSTERS RIGHT AWAY.

NOW I WAS STUPIDLY BORN IN MAY, SO THAT I HAD TO WAIT FOR AGES BEFORE

THERE WAS AN "R" IN THE MONTH,
AND I COULD ENJOY THE GOOD THINGS
OF LIFE SUCH AS PORK SAUSAGES,
AND PARTRIDGES AND PERSIMMONS.
THE HEAD CAT
HAS WRITTEN A BOOK
ABOUT HIS FAMILY
WHICH BIDS FAIR TO
EAT THE RABBITS
AT MULTIPLICATION
AND I AM SENDING
YOU A COPY SO THAT
YOU CAN FOLLOW THEIR
ADVENTURES. THE
LAZY FELLOW HAS
FORGOTTEN TO COLOUR
THE ILLUSTRATIONS SO
I GOT MR DAVEY TO PUT
IN A PAINT BOX, SO
THAT YOU CAN REMEDY HIS DEFICIENCIES.
WE WENT OFF TO MANOEUVRES

ON THE PLAIN ON THE 7TH AND
ARE NOW AT TIDWORTH PARK. I
FOUND QUITE A NICE HOTEL FOR
MY EVENING GLASS OF BEER, AND
THOUGHT AT FIRST THEY'D CALLED
IT AFTER ME BUT AFTER
I'D HAD A
TANKARD OR
TWO, AND PUT
ON MY GLASSES
I FOUND IT
WAS ONLY THE
"BUSTARD".
(SOME MULE IN
"B" SUBSECTION
I
SUPPOSE.)

WE HAD A GREAT
NIGHT IN THE MESS
WITH THE "TERRIERS"
JUST BEFORE WE LEFT
EWSHOTT, AND AS WE
REGULARS ARE DOING ALL WE CAN

TO HELP THEM THIS YEAR I GAVE THEM
SOME EQUITATION LESSONS AND
TAUGHT THEM HOW TO DISMOUNT.
I HAD FOUR OF THEM ON THE
FLOOR AT ONCE AND WE ALL
HAD GREAT ENJOYMENT.

YOUR LOVING

CHS

R. A. MESS,

EWSHOTT CAMP,

Nᴿ ALDERSHOT,

HANTS.

4ᵀᴴ DECEMBER 1930

MY DEAR BRIGHTIE

As I WAS PACKING UP MY HOUSEHOLD GODS, AND GETTING READY FOR THE MOVE TO BULFORD TOMORROW,

I FOUND MY BIRTHDAY BOOK AND SAW I HAD NEARLY FORGOTTEN YOUR BIRTHDAY. I WAS SO UPSET THAT I ATE ALL THE PACKING STRAW BEFORE I CAME ROUND. ALL MY DRAWING MATERIALS HAD GONE OFF WITH THE HEAVY BAGGAGE THIS MORNING SO I HAD TO COME ROUND TO THE MESS TO SEE WHAT I COULD FIND.

LAST TIME I DINED IN THE MESS I HAD AN NASTY WHISKER AS A SALAD

AND MR DAVEY WASN'T A BIT BUCKED WHEN IT FELL OFF THE WHAT-NOT, AND BROKE THE VASE. I REALLY DIDN'T WANT TO GO HOME AT ALL THAT NIGHT, IT WAS SO COLD THAT I WAS SURE IT WAS FREEZING. I COULD HEAR THE ICE CRACKLING UNDER MY FEET IN THE PUDDLES, AND HAD QUITE AN ARGUMENT ABOUT IT — BUT MR DAVEY SAID

I WAS WALKING ALL OVER HIS
CUCUMBER
FRAMES.

I DIDN'T BELIEVE HIM AT THE TIME, BUT THE
BILL I GOT FOR BROKEN WINDOWS BEFORE
MARCHING OUT MADE AN AWFUL HOLE IN
MY MONEY BOX.

I DON'T KNOW WHAT I'M GOING TO
DO ABOUT CHRISTMAS PRESENTS, BECAUSE
AFTER BUYING THE STAMP FOR THIS
I'VE ONLY $7\frac{1}{2}$D LEFT.

BEST OF LOVE, AND MANY HAPPY RETURNS
OF THE DAY FROM
Your LOVING

Cus

TELEGRAPHIC ADDRESS,
RAG, PICCY, LONDON.
TELEPHONE, GERRARD 9721-8.

ARMY & NAVY CLUB,
PALL MALL. S.W.1.

23RD DECEMBER 1930

MY DEAR MERRIE & BRIGHT

I DO HOPE YOU'LL BOTH HAVE A VERY HAPPY CHRISTMAS WITH LOTS OF NICE PRESENTS AND TURKEYS AND YORKSHIRE PUDDING BUT I WISH YOU WERE COMING TO SEE ME ON CHRISTMAS DAY.

THIS YEAR I HAD SUCH A GOOD IDEA. I BORROWED ONE OF DELLA'S GYM STOCKINGS (THE LONG SORT

IN WHICH SHE DOES HER SLIMMING EXERCISES

BEFORE SHE GOES IN FOR THE SHOW
AND I'M SURE THEY CAN PUT MASSES
OF PRESENTS IN TO IT.

    I HAD TO COME UP TO
LONDON TO DO MY SHOPPING AS
YOU CAN'T GET ANYTHING AT BULFORD.
    I DON'T KNOW WHAT WE SHALL DO
THERE, UNLESS WE PRACTICE DRUIDICAL RITES
AT THE SUMMER SOLSTICE, BUT WE'RE

MUCH MORE LIKELY TO BE PRACTICING BRIGADE
CONCENTRATIONS AT LARK HILL ON THAT
DATE.

ARMY & NAVY CLUB,
PALL MALL. S.W.1.

WELL, AS I WAS SAYING — BEFORE I INTERPRETED MYSELF — I CAME UP TO TOWN TO DO MY CHRISTMAS SHOPPING AND HAD TEA AT THE "RAG" OF COURSE THAT'S A CLUB FOR GENTLEMEN ONLY BUT THEY

HAVE A LADIES ROOM TO MAKE IT MORE SOCIABLE. THAT'S HOW I GOT HOLD OF THIS

PAPER. I EXPECTED THE PLACE TO BE FULL OF GENERALS AND ADMIRALS WITH THE PLUMES WAVING FROM THEIR FORAGE CAPS AND THEIR CHESTS ALL OVER FROGS AND MEDALS – LIKE YOU READ ABOUT – BUT REALLY IF IT WASN'T FOR THE CONVERSATION YOU'D NEVER KNOW THEY WERE'NT JUST LIKE YOU AND ME.

DID Mr DAVIE TELL YOU I WAS MADE AN HONOURABLE MEMBER. OF THE MESS AT BULFORD ON THE FIRST WEDNESDAY AFTER WE GOT THERE.

I SIMPLY JUMPED FOR JOY, AND FOUR
OFFICERS OF THE EQUITATION SCHOOL
WHO WERE ON MY BACK FELL OFF.
THEY MADE QUITE A BIG HEAP ON
THE FLOOR.

NOW I MUST CATCH THE TRAIN
BACK

EVER YOUR,
LOVING

CUS

R.A. MESS,
BULFORD CAMP,
SALISBURY.
TELEPHONE 89 BULFORD

2ND FEBRUARY 1931

MY DEAR BRIGHTIE

THE OTHER DAY WHILE I
WAS WORKING, TRYING TO
PLANT A NICE CROP OF
LETTUCES, AND THISTLES, AND
OTHER USEFUL THINGS LIKE
TINS AND DEAD CATS (FOR
I CAN'T BEAR WASTE AND
UNTIDYNESS) IN THE MAJOR'S
GARDEN, THE POSTMAN
BROUGHT ME YOUR LETTER,
AND I HAD TO RUN OFF
TO THE RECREATION ROOM
TO GET MY GLASSES TO
READ IT.
IT WAS SNOWING HARD,

OUTSIDE , SO I TOOK TWO GLASSES , LIKE TIMOTHY , FOR MY STOMACH'S SAKE.

I'M VERY SORRY TO HEAR THAT KITTY'S PUPPY IS SO NAUGHTY AS TO WISH TO ESCAPE FROM THE DOLLS PRAM, WHICH I SHOULD HAVE THOUGHT A VERY ELEGANT MODE OF PROGRESSION.

CAN'T YOU TELL HIM ITS AN AUTO CAR , WHICH OUGHT TO GO IF IT HAD AN ENGINE. HE CAN'T REALLY BE OLD ENOUGH TO GO IN A MOTOR BY HIMSELF LIKE KITTY AND BUSTER.

MR DAVEY'S "JACK" HAS HURT HIS EYE , WHICH MAKES HIS EXPRESSION MORE MALIGNANT THAN EVER. HE NOW HAS ONE EYE LOOKING TO THE EAST WHILE THE OTHER LOOKS NORTH , AND THE RESULT IS MOST DISTRACTING WHEN YOU ARE TALKING TO HIM.

THE HEAD CAT STAYED BEHIND AT
EWSHOTT AS HE SAID HE COULDN'T
AFFORD TO MOVE HIS FAMILY, BUT
MINNIE, THE SADDLER'S TORTOISESHELL
BROUGHT HER TWO SANDY KITTENS IN
A TEA CHEST. TWO VERY LONG
HAIRED TABBIES HAVE ALSO BEEN TAKEN
ON THE STRENGTH.

I DON'T LIKE
THIS PLACE AS
MUCH AS EWSHOTT
WITH ALL THE
WOODS AND WILLOWS
AND

OWLS

AND SQUIRRELS. HERE THERE ARE ONLY
RABBITS AND SHEEP, AND THE SHEEP HAVE
SUCH SILLY FACES THAT YOU CAN'T EXPECT
ANY REALLY INTELLIGENT CONVERSATION
FROM THEM.

THE FORAGE IS NOT WHAT IT.
OUGHT TO BE EITHER, AND ON THE

WINTER SCALE WE ONLY GET ONE AND
A HALF RUGS A MONTH, INSTEAD OF
ONE A FORTNIGHT. I CALL IT

DOWN RIGHT
MEAN,
AND AM
SURE THE
LABOUR
GOVERNMENT
IS RESPONSIBLE
FOR
IMPAIRING OUR
EFFICIENCY.
I'D WRITE TO
THE "TIMES"

ABOUT IT, IF I WASN'T SURE THAT THEY
ONLY READ THE "DAILY HERALD".

YOUR LOVING

CUS

R. A. MESS,
BULFORD CAMP,
SALISBURY.
TELEPHONE 89 BULFORD.

2ND APRIL 1931

MY DEAR MARRIE

AND

BRIGHT

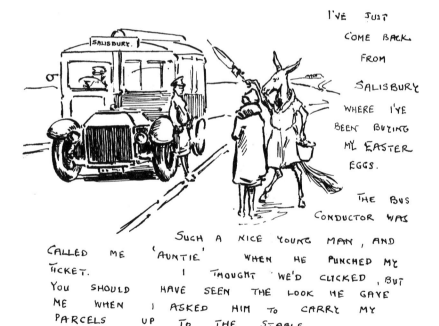

I'VE JUST COME BACK FROM SALISBURY WHERE I'VE BEEN BUYING MY EASTER EGGS.

THE BUS CONDUCTOR WAS SUCH A NICE YOUNG MAN, AND CALLED ME 'AUNTIE' WHEN HE PUNCHED MY TICKET. I THOUGHT WE'D CLICKED, BUT YOU SHOULD HAVE SEEN THE LOOK HE GAVE ME WHEN I ASKED HIM TO CARRY MY PARCELS UP TO THE STABLE.

I EXPECT HE BELONGS TO ONE OF THOSE MECHANISED BATTERIES AND GETS HIS MANNERS FROM A CARDEN-LLOYD.

ALL THE HARES ON THE PLAIN HAVE GONE MAD, AND ARE BUSY MAKING EASTER EGGS, SO WE'VE GIVEN UP HUNTING THEM TO MAKE JUGGED HARE, AND LAST SATURDAY WE BORROWED A REAL STAG FROM THE

BERKS AND BUCKS AND CHASED HIM INSTEAD.

WHEN THE JELLY DOGS FIRST GOT THE SCENT THEY DIDN'T KNOW WHAT TO DO, BECAUSE THEY DIDN'T KNOW WHAT WAS AT THE OTHER END OF THE SMELL, BUT THEN "OLD BILL" JOINED IN.

HE'S NOT AN ORDINARY HOUND AT ALL, BUT AN ALSADOR (FATHER - ALSATIAN WOLF HOUND - VERY HIGH CLASS MOTHER - LABRADOR RATHER DECLASSÉE) WELL HE KNEW ALL ABOUT VENISON, SO WENT OFF ON

A HUNT OF HIS OWN, AND THE HOUNDS WERE SO JEALOUS AT HIS GETTING AWAY WITHOUT THEM THAT THEY STARTED HUNTING HIM.

AND THEN IT ALL GOT VERY CONFUSED. I FOUND THE STAG DRINKING IN THE STONEHENGE INN, AND WE SAT AND LAUGHED AT THE OTHER DOGS CHASING OLD BILL ROUND STONE HENGE ITSELF.

I DID LIKE BRIGHT'S LAST LETTER, AND IT MADE ME LAUGH, BUT I WISH YOU'D BOTH COME BACK TO THE BATTERY AS I HARDLY EVER GET ANY SUGAR ON SUNDAY MORNINGS NOW. THEY MAKE EVERYBODY GO TO CHURCH ON SUNDAYS HERE AND I THINK IT'S VERY GOOD FOR CORA. ONLY THE FIRST SIX ROWS OF SEATS HAVE FOOTSTOOLS, AND A LOT OF THE MULES ARE GETTING BIG KNEES LIKE MINE. EVEN BOBBIE HAS 'HOUSEMAID'S KNEE', AND I DON'T THINK WE'LL SHOW HIM THIS YEAR.

CUSTARD

BEST WISHES FOR A VERY HAPPY
EASTER AND LOTS OF OATS IN
YOUR BRAN

Your Loving

Gus

R.A. MESS,
BULFORD CAMP,
SALISBURY.
TELEPHONE 89 BULFORD.

7TH JUNE 1931

MY DEAR MERRIE & BRIGHT

I HAVE BEEN TOO BUSY WITH TRAINING TO WRITE SINCE EASTER BUT THIS IS A WET SUNDAY AND I CAN'T BEAR THE THOUGHT OF RUINING MY ASCOT FROCK GOING TO CHURCH.

IT'S SO SMART PUCE ALPACA WITH A MUSLIN FRILL AND JUST SUITS MY COMPLEXION.

WE HAD A FARMERS' DINNER IN THE MESS
A MONTH AGO AND I GAVE THEM ALL
RIDES — THREE OR FOUR AT A TIME

IT WAS THE GREATEST FUN FOR IN TEN
SECONDS THEY WERE ALL CLINGING TO THE
ROOF BEAMS FESTOONED LIKE MONKEYS. I
THINK THERE MUST HAVE BEEN A DOZEN
OF THEM HANGING UP AT ONCE, BUT I
HAVE ONLY DRAWN TWO AS SAMPLES

THEN WE HAD THE HORSE SHOW ON
18TH MAY. NOT SO GOOD AS THE
ALDERSHOT ONE, BUT WE DID VERY WELL
WE PUT IN TWO GUN TEAMS, AND
TOOK 1ST AND 2ND PRIZES.

THE HEAD OF THE ARMY HERE WAS SO PLEASED THAT WHEN WE CAME IN FRONT OF THE GRAND STAND TO GET OUR PRIZES HE TOLD THE PUBLIC THEY MUST COME IN AND GET A 'CLOSE UP' OF US, AND THEY SWARMED ALL ROUND THE TEAMS FOR QUITE TWENTY MINUTES.

"BABY" GOT 1ST PRIZE FOR MULES (£2) AND STOOD US CARROTS ALL ROUND WHEN HE GOT BACK. HE GAVE ME A BOTTLE OF BEER, FOR MY TUMMY'S SAKE AS IT WAS A COLD DAY

DICK WAS 2ND PRIZE AND CARMEN WAS HIGHLY COMMENDED. SHE BELONGS TO "C" SUB AND EXCHANGED WITH OLD CROKE WHO WANTED TO STAY AT ALDERSHOT FOR FAMILY REASONS. YOU SEE WE LEFT THE FARRIER BEHIND, WHERE "CROKE" BIT HIM, SO WE HAD TO LEAVE "CROKE" TO KEEP HIM IN ORDER, AND SEE THAT HE DID HIS WORK.

OLD "DELLA" GOT NOTHING THIS YEAR AND IS AWFULLY CROSS ABOUT IT.

MR DAVEY WAS MADE A CAPTAIN YESTERDAY SO I SHALL HAVE TO TOUCH MY HAT TO HIM IN THE MORNING.

YOUR LOVING

Gus.

24ᵀᴴ MARCH 1932

My DEAR

MERRIE AND BRIGHT

I'VE HAD SUCH A HECTIC
WEEK THAT I REALLY
DON'T KNOW THE
COOKHOUSE FROM THE
CORN BIN, OR MY
FEED TIN FROM CORA'S
FOR THAT MATTER.

I MEANT TO TELEPHONE
TO INVITE YOU OVER ON
SUNDAY, BUT THE KING
YET SAID HE WANTED TO
SEE US AT A MOMENT'S
NOTICE, AND IT UPSET ALL
MY ARRANGEMENTS.

IT KNOCKED ALL MY 18 DAY DIET
AND SLIMMING EXERCISES ON THE HEAD, FOR

151

HE'S ONE OF THE SORT THAT ADMIRES CURVES.
OF COURSE BABY WAS ALL RIGHT, FOR
HE'S PACKED WITH BRAN, LIKE A DOLL

BUT "DELLA"

AND I

HAVE TO

CONSIDER OUR

FIGURES

IF WE ARE

GOING TO ASCOT

THIS YEAR.

WE'D VERY

LITTLE TIME

BUT

PLENTY OF MATERIAL — SO WE JUST PACKED
THREE RUGS EACH INSIDE US, AND

FAIRLY CAUGHT
THE JUDGE'S
EYE, AS WE
FILED PAST.
I ALWAYS HEARD

GENTLEMEN PREFERRED BLONDES, BUT DO YOU

KNOW HE ACTUALLY PICKED OUT DELLA, RATHER THAN ME, SO I CONSIDER HE'S NO GENTLEMAN.

ON WEDNESDAY WE DID A DEMONSTRATION FOR THE NAVY. THAT'S THE SORT OF SHOW TO BE IN. THE MEN DO ALL THE DONKEY WORK, AND THE MULES HAVE NOTHING TO DO BUT SIT IN THE WARD ROOM AND DRINK HORSES' NECKS. I'D HAVE A PETROL PUMP INSTALLED THOUGH, AS THEIR GLASSES GET BROKEN SO EASILY. BESIDES IT WOULD BE LESS TROUBLE THAN GETTING UP SO OFTEN TO RING FOR THE WAITER, OR STEWARD OR WHATEVER THEY CALL THE STABLE MAN.

I'M THINKING OF APPLYING FOR A TRANSFER
ON COMPASSIONATE GROUNDS, FOR I CAN'T
STAND MUCH MORE OF THIS "PLAIN". IF
IT WAS FLAT I WOULDN'T MIND, BUT
THESE LONG, ROLLING SLOPES
MAKE ME FEEL
JUST LIKE AN ANT
ON A SHEET
     OF

CORRUGATED

      IRON.

   THE ONLY COMPENSATION
      IS THE RABBITS, WHICH
         REMINDS ME THAT I FOUND
            ONE FOR LYDIA AS
               AN EASTER EGG.

               YOUR LOVING

                  CUS

1ST APRIL 1932

MY DEAR MERRIE & BRIGHT

I WENT IN FOR A RACE THE OTHER DAY, AND CAME IN LAST. I REALLY THINK I SHOULD HAVE BEEN PLACED FIRST, FOR I HAD TO RUN BACKWARDS ALL THE WAY TO SAVE MY KNEE.

AND LOOK ROUND AT EACH FENCE TO SEE WHERE I WAS JUMPING. THOUGH I WAS LEPPING

LIKE A FROG IT WAS A GREAT HANDICAP
AND CAPTAIN DAVIE WOULDN'T PUT HIS
SHIRT ON ME, WHICH I THOUGHT SHOWED
A LACK OF CONFIDENCE. I HAD
TO PUT MY CHEMISE ON, AND NOW THE
POOR OLD GOVERNMENT IS ANOTHER RUG
DOWN.

YOUR EASTER EGGS CAME
JUST IN TIME TO SAVE
MY LIFE.

I ATE MERRIE'S
ON EASTER
MORNING, AND
IT WAS
SCRUMPTIOUS.

THEN I HAD
A BRIGHT IDEA
ABOUT BRIGHT'S.

I THOUGHT IF I
HATCHED IT OUT I
MIGHT GET A CHOCOLATE RABBIT.

SO I  GOT SOME STRAW AND
CONSTRUCTED
A
MARE'S NEST
IN
MY STALL.
THEN I TOOK MY
KNITTING, AND
SAT THERE
TILL TUESDAY
AFTERNOON, WHEN
THE MAJOR CAME BACK, AND CALLED ME
AN OLD FOOL — BUT PERHAPS HE
MEANT MULE. HE SAID I'D BE
LUCKY IF I FOUND ANYONE ELSE TO
PUT UP WITH MY ABSURDITIES, WHEN
HE WENT TO CHINA

ANYHOW HE HAS PROMISED THAT

I SHALL BE ATTACHED TO THE OFFICERS'
MESS DURING MANOEUVRES AND SHALL BE

ENTITLED TO DRAW MY BEER AS USUAL.

I HOPE THE NEW MAJOR WON'T TAKE IT IN THE LITERAL SENSE, IN THE WAY I HAVE DRAWN IT ON THE LAST PAGE, BUT I HAVE GREAT FAITH IN CAPTAIN DAVIE STANDING UP FOR MY RIGHTS — THOUGH HE'S ONLY AN ADJUTANT NOW. GREATER MEN HAVE SUNK AS LOW, BUT I DON'T DESPAIR OF SEEING HIM AS CAPTAIN OF A MULE BATTERY YET, AND THEN EVEN I WOULD GET A PRIZE, IF IT WERE ONLY FOR GOOD CONDUCT.

YOUR LOVING

CUS

Biographical Note

Valentine Rodolphe Burkhardt, the son of a Swiss silk merchant and an English mother, was born in 1884. From Clifton College he joined the Army and at 19 was commissioned into the Royal Field Artillery. In 1912 he married Edith Elspeth Ewing; they had a daughter, Elspeth, born in 1913, and a son, John, in 1916. In 1913 Lieutenant Burkhardt went as a Language Student to Peking and qualified as a First Class Interpreter in Mandarin.

Recalled for the First World War, he served a year as Staff Captain R.A. 28th Division in France and Belgium. In November, 1915, he went as Deputy Assistant Adjutant and Quartermaster General 42nd Division to the Mediterranean Expeditionary Force (Greek Macedonia, Serbia, Bulgaria, European Turkey and the Aegean Islands). The Allied attempt to dislodge the Turks from the Gallipoli peninsula had petered out after much loss of life. In April, 1915, Merrie and Bright's father, Lieutenant Middleton, had arrived in the Mediterranean from India. His ship had been torpedoed and he had spent four hours in the water before continuing to Gallipoli in the *River Clyde*. Believed to be the first Gunner officer to reach the shore alive, he had been severely wounded, part of his left arm being shattered. The Secretary of State for War, Field-Marshal Lord Kitchener, after a personal inspection in November, 1915, recommended evacuation of the British, French and Anzac troops deployed there. In December, with the temporary rank of Major, Burkhardt was sent to assist in the arrangements for this, which was carried out in one month, without the loss of a single life and to the complete surprise of the Turkish enemy. Burkhardt left the peninsula on 1 January, 1916, probably with the rest of his Division, and was mentioned in despatches on that date, presumably for his part in the evacuation.

On 12 January he arrived in Egypt and continued serving as 42nd Division's DAA and QMG and later as Deputy Assistant Adjutant General to the Expeditionary Force there. The Division took part in the Suez and Sinai campaigns against the Turks and crossed the Sinai desert as far as the border with Palestine.

In February, 1917, Burkhardt left for France, almost certainly as part of an advance Staff party to prepare for the arrival there of his Division. He reached the Western Front in April, was awarded the DSO (gazetted on 21 June), again mentioned in despatches on 6 July and confirmed in the rank of Major. By August, 1917, 42nd Division was part of the British force holding the line during the Third Battle of Ypres, commonly known as Passchendaele, after the village and ridge which formed primary objectives for the British and Empire troops during the battle. When what remained of the village was finally taken on 6 November by the Canadians, the entire battlefield had been reduced to a sea of muddy craters after the most appalling losses — 300,000 men killed and wounded, missing or made prisoner.

From 9 January, 1918, till 21 October, 1919, he served as General Staff Officer Grade 2, first as liaison officer with the French army and then with the British Mission at the Headquarters of the Allied Commander-in-Chief, Marshal Foch. He was again mentioned in despatches in December, 1918, and awarded the Légion d'Honneur 5th Class and the Croix de Guerre. Meanwhile the Burkhardts' marriage had ended in separation; neither remarried.

From 1920 till 1923 Major Burkhardt was a member of the Interallied Commission of Control, Germany. In 1923 he returned to China as a G.S.O.2. and spent five years in Tientsin, travelling extensively in the interior during his tour of duty. Then followed four years' regimental service at home commanding the 13th Light Battery, 5th Light Brigade R.A., first at Ewshott, then at Bulford.

In 1932 Burkhardt was appointed Military Attaché in Peking and was joined by his daughter who acted as his hostess. Promoted to Colonel in 1935, for a short time he commanded the 7th Heavy Brigade, The Western Defences in Singapore. In 1936 he was back as G.S.O.1. at China Command, Hong Kong; he was retired in 1939, but recalled as Military Attaché to the British Embassy, which was now alternating between Shanghai and Chungking, until 1941 when, on his final retirement from the Army, he and his daughter returned to the U.K. From 1943-1946 he was employed by the the Navy.

After some time spent with his son and daughter-in-law, Burkhardt retired to Hong Kong. He had met in Peking Madame Natasha de Breuil, who was now also living in Hong Kong and had a shop selling books on old China and Chinese objets d'art. She introduced him to the 'boat people', the junkmen in whose lives and customs they were both deeply interested and involved. With her collaboration he wrote and illustrated three books on Chinese Creeds and Customs which was published in three volumes. He was also an acknowledged authority on butterflies and painted the butterflies of Hong Kong to illustrate an article for the Journal of the Hong Kong branch of the Royal Asiatic Society. He also added to his father's collection of old Chinese stamps and illlustrated the albums most beautifully. He died in 1967.

Note by M.A.M.J. *I have compiled these biographical notes from Colonel Burkhardt's Army Records, his entry in* Who Was Who, *his obituary notice in the* R.A. Regimental News, *and two letters to my mother from V.R.B. in 1964 and 1966. Toby Buchan kindly provided the military and historical background behind the bare dates and places quoted in V.R.B.'s Army records for the First World War.*